OV

Overdue

A Dewey Decimal System of Grace

Valerie Schultz

A *Give Us This Day* Book

LITURGICAL PRESS
Collegeville, Minnesota

www.litpress.org

Cover design by Amy Marc. Illustration courtesy of iStock by Getty Images.

Portions of some of the essays in this book previously appeared in THE BAKERSFIELD CALIFORNIAN, AMERICA, HUMAN DEVELOPMENT, LIGUORIAN, and THE LEVAN HUMANITIES REVIEW.

Names have been changed to respect privacy.

1	2	3	4	5	6	7	8	9

Library of Congress Cataloging-in-Publication Data

Names: Schultz, Valerie, author.
Title: Overdue : a Dewey decimal system of grace / Valerie Schultz.
Description: Collegeville : Liturgical Press, 2019. | Summary: "Valerie Schultz shares what she learned and the grace she received during fourteen years working inside an American prison"— Provided by publisher.
Identifiers: LCCN 2019012523 (print) | ISBN 9780814664117 (pbk.)
Subjects: LCSH: Church work with prisoners. | Prison libraries—Miscellanea.
Classification: LCC BV4465 .S364 2019 (print) | LCC BV4465 (ebook) | DDC 259/.5—dc23
LC record available at https://lccn.loc.gov/2019012523
LC ebook record available at https://lccn.loc.gov/2019980012

For the Men of Facility D

300 Social Sciences

400 Language

500 Pure Science

600 Technology

Introduction

When I was in prison, you visited me." Hearing these words from the Gospel of Matthew many times while growing up, I never imagined they would one day describe me. I never imagined that I would visit a prison, much less spend time with prisoners. I lived for eighteen years in a California community that included a prison within its boundaries before I ever went inside one. Prison was dangerous. Nothing good ever happened in there.

The way I started as a volunteer facilitating Catholic Communion services was an O. Henry-like story of a mix-up of ministry meetings at the local parish. I had recently resigned from a parish position and was at loose ends spiritually. Two new ministries were starting up at the time: a St. Vincent de Paul chapter and a detention ministry group. My husband volunteered us for St. Vincent de Paul, but the same woman, Emma, was taking sign-ups for both groups. Emma mistakenly told me that my husband had signed us up for detention ministry. This kind of freaked me out, conjuring up every book and movie I'd ever seen that dramatized the terror of prison.

"Emma called to remind us about the detention ministry group organizational meeting," I told my husband, hesitantly, one evening.

"Oh. Ohhh-kaaay," my husband said with a similar hesitation. Curiously, we didn't discuss it any further. We both went to the meeting in secret trepidation, each thinking that we were supporting our mate's out-of-the-blue calling. Was it odd or was it God?

Long story short, we went "inside" and were blessed beyond measure. We'd expected the inmates to be scarier, like characters

from central casting, but the reality was that they were just
folks—young, old, short, tall, thin, stout, bald, well-coiffed,
English-speaking, Spanish-speaking, outgoing, shy, articulate,
silent, funny, stern. While they were sometimes tattooed to an
alarming extent, they possessed all the quirks and gifts and
flaws, the nobility and the sin, that define humanity. The men
we met in prison profoundly enriched our lives. They gave us
much more than we gave them.

As my stint in prison developed from volunteering to working in a clerical position to running a library on a yard, I came
to see the prisoners more each day as human beings, created
by and beloved of God. For the most part, the men I dealt with
were respectful and even considerate. Some, of course, were
certifiably psychopathic; some were mean or misogynistic;
some had fallen in with a gang; some were actually innocent
of the crime for which they'd been convicted; some had done
something stupid and regrettable; some were addicts and alcoholics. In short, they were much like the non-incarcerated
population. My fourteen years inside were a time of grace and
learning. It was no challenge to find God in all things in prison,
because God was palpably everywhere.

I think of re-imagining our prisons as places for rehabilitation—an ideal that our present criminal justice system does
not meet—not only as a political struggle but as a spiritual
one. Along with being disproportionately handed to people
of color and people of limited monetary means, prison time
is mainly punitive. Taxpayers often see no need to provide
inmates with any services beyond those necessary for physical
survival. Many people think that, as ugly as prison time may
be, these transgressors deserve whatever they get. They should
be thoroughly and satisfyingly punished: justice as retribution
rather than any kind of restoration. And anyone who has ever
been the victim of a crime understandably wants the perpetra-

tor of their suffering to suffer in equal measure. I totally get that deeply human response to being hurt, and I have been there myself. I know the thirst for revenge. Compassion for the convicted is not easy to come by.

This book is not an academic study of prison issues. It is a witnessing of sorts. I do hope to prompt an engagement in some soul-searching about our criminal justice priorities and policies, about the racism and classism they perpetuate, and about revamping the system to lift our fellow sinners up to healing and wholeness.

I have organized these essays around the Dewey Decimal System of book cataloging to honor the prison library where it was my privilege to work and to partake of God's grace in many forms. The Dewey Decimal System has been largely replaced by the Library of Congress cataloging system, but smaller collections, like those in elementary schools or prisons, still utilize Dewey. Life is rarely so well organized as Dewey, but we can dream. I also ask the reader to keep in mind a prison maxim: "Today's inmate is tomorrow's neighbor." This may alarm us, but it's true: most inmates will be released back into the community. Most intend to fit into society. Most know that the deck is stacked against them. Most can be rehabilitated. And most will respond to a kind word or an extended hand.

We can be good neighbors to anyone the good Lord plops down next to us. We can be the face of Jesus no matter where we work or live. We can be part of the solution, which is, always and of course, love.

Here's the Deal

The first time I walked into the library that would be my home away from home for the next five years, I noticed the windows. Soaring up to the high ceiling, the bank of windows at the south end of the unexpectedly large and spacious room admitted the spring morning light in a way that made me feel like I'd come home. Dust motes diffused themselves in the sun's rays, as I saw with surprise that the room looked much more like a library than a penal institution. Of course, that impression was countered by the rows of uncomfortable-looking orange plastic chairs flanking low, heavy, mismatched wooden tables that had been built decades ago in the Carpentry vocational shop by inmates no longer around, not to mention the cages encasing the few windows that actually opened. The room, devoid of patrons, smelled like books. More precisely, it smelled like a secondhand bookstore. I learned later that this library was unusual for a prison because it had open stacks the inmates could browse. Most prison libraries, constructed after this dinosaur of a prison, were small rooms with closed stacks; all books were behind a counter and the patrons could only choose their reading material from an inventory list. This library was unusually bookish. On the shelves that lined the walls and formed aisles down the middle of the large room, there must have been ten thousand volumes, their mysterious wisdom beckoning.

But no humans were there to respond to the call of the books. The library was empty. For months, it had been open only rarely, due to a lack of staff and a statewide hiring freeze. I had been transferred from another position under a special dispensation from Sacramento. The prison library must be functional, because the law mandates that the California Department of Corrections and Rehabilitation (CDCR) provide its charges meaningful access to the courts. So inmates in California are guaranteed at least two hours per week for the purpose of pursuing their own legal work, four hours if they can show a verifiable court deadline within thirty days. The law also assures their access to recreational reading materials, like books, newspapers, and magazines.

The legal side of the library included computer terminals loaded with massive files of legal statutes and court decisions, as well as bookcases crammed with traditional law books in print, and the necessary county, state, and federal forms to file legal actions when acting as one's own attorney. Which was the case with most of the law patrons. Some of them might be working on appeals or motions for resentencing or civil lawsuits or filing writs of habeas corpus (which my beginner legal brain translated as "show me the body!"). Some might be preparing for parole board hearings. Some might be fighting for custody of their children or going through divorce proceedings. The library was the place for legal research and resources, including forms, envelopes, copies, and commiseration.

On the recreational reading side of the library were current and back issues of magazines and newspapers, various reference volumes, and fiction and nonfiction books. The magazines stayed in the library and, I soon learned, had to be monitored to discourage the surreptitious ripping out of pages featuring beautiful women or sports heroes. The books could be checked out two at a time. The security level of this particular facility permitted hardback books; some higher levels did not, and library staff there had to remove any hard covers, because they were considered "weapon stock." Some of the library books were purchased through the state budget, and some were donated, by prisoners or by kind strangers. Some were fairly recent, and some had filled these shelves for a long time.

Before my appointment, the skeletal staff of the prison's education department had been barely meeting the legal requirements for a functioning library for several months. Teachers had been pulled from their classrooms to open the library for an hour here and there, doing the minimum of checking out books and providing court forms and making legal copies. The teachers, as one might imagine, were unhappy about this task. Now it was my job to get this library open and running, mainly so that the inmates' complaints and legal appeals would stop. I was also charged with opening another library on the minimum security yard in the same prison, which was also unstaffed and hardly ever open. I would spend three days a week on my home yard and two days at the minimum yard, until more staff could be hired.

Both of these yards at the time were designated as a "Sensitive Needs Yard," or SNY. Prisoners who wouldn't fare well on a General Population (GP) yard were housed here for their own safety. The SNY population was mostly composed of sex offenders, homosexual or transgender inmates, "snitches," those whose offenses had harmed children or the elderly, and gang dropouts. SNYs were unusual for their racial mix, because unlike on the strictly self-segregated GP yards, SNY inmates had to agree to live alongside those with whom they disagreed or who might even be their former enemies. (SNYs were not without their own unique problems, and the CDCR has since discontinued the designation in favor of "programming" yards.)

After two days of training, courtesy of a staff library aide on loan from another prison, I was on my own. Well, not exactly on my own, as I had six inmate clerks on each yard under my supervision. I already knew some of the inmates on both yards from my time as a Catholic volunteer, but I didn't know any of these guys. And they didn't know me. And so the dance began.

Although the inmates referred to me as "the librarian-lady," I was not a librarian, as I lacked a master's degree in Library Science. My job title was Library Technical Assistant, or LTA. But I was in charge of the medium-security library, and I planned to make it the most positive and generative place it could be under the circumstances. I wanted it to be an oasis, a little patch of serenity within the strictures of the institution.

The job duties of the inmate library assistants, or clerks, were to check books in and out, reshelve and repair books, monitor the door as patrons signed in and out, provide customer service at the legal counter, and clean the library every morning. They'd done their jobs for way longer than I had done mine, and they were delighted to be back at work full-time after the long shutdown time. But they were still figuring out what my deal was, meaning what kind of boss I was going to be.

I had taken in so much information in my two training days and had made copious notes, but I soon found that the reality of supervising inmates and serving the eager and deprived library patrons on each yard was of more immediate concern than differentiating between the forms for the civil and criminal courts. I was surprised and pleased by the high level of legal expertise among the clerks. In their capacity as paid clerks, they were not supposed to dispense legal advice or to accept any extra recompense for their services apart from their state wages. (Their pay, upon being hired, was fifteen cents an hour. They topped out at thirty-two cents an hour. My total monthly payroll for each yard was never more than two hundred dollars: our tax dollars at work.) Inmates could, however, help each other as peers, and there were known "jailhouse lawyers" on both yards.

Allow me to make your acquaintance with some of the clerks who worked in the library over the years. Here, and throughout the book, their names and some biographical details have been changed to respect their privacy. (I usually called my clerks by their first names, a habit carried over from my time as a religious volunteer, even though a sergeant once roared at me, "WHAT is every inmate's first name? INMATE!")

Neil, the savviest law clerk ever, turned sixty during his time in the library. He was a lifer. A life sentence is not necessarily life without the possibility of parole, known as LWOP, but can be 15-to-life, or 25-to-life, or something-to-life, which is how the court builds a tiny possibility of freedom into the sentence. Neil had already served decades of his term. He was a former heroin addict who had unintentionally run over and killed a person during a robbery. He was given to hyperbole and was never shy about expressing his opinion. Regarding legal matters, Neil was self-educated and usually right. He probably could have passed the bar exam. He had a natural curiosity and was always looking to learn, especially about technology. As the traditional print law books were in the process of being phased out in favor of computer-based legal resources, Neil took it upon himself to encourage the other old timers to familiarize themselves with the legal research computers. He patiently taught many men who had never touched a computer how to navigate the rivers of information available therein. Neil had married and divorced a pen pal at least once while he'd been incarcerated but had never had children. He was a father figure to many of the younger inmates, though, steering them through the choppy waters of their legal appeals and motions and writs. I often saw Neil on one side of a table listening intently to an inmate seated on the other side, his head bowed like he was hearing a confession. And maybe in a way he was: Neil the priest needed a true account of the inmate's misdeeds before he could direct him to possible legal recourse. Neil, not making eye contact as he listened, used an old parenting trick: kids open up more if you appear to be looking elsewhere. When Neil was finally found suitable for parole, after many unsuccessful appearances before the parole board, he left prison and rejoined a society he hardly recognized. A life-long learner, he soon discovered Facebook. That's how he reconnected with his high school sweetheart and married her.

George was a former leader of a Latino gang. He had spent many years in solitary confinement on account of the gang activity he'd continued even after he'd gone to prison for dealing drugs. He'd finally left the gang, been debriefed by prison authorities, and worked his way down to a minimum security SNY. Three things he told me about solitary have stayed with me: that the 24/7 fluorescent lighting had permanently messed with his eyesight, that he had talked to himself in two languages to keep from going mad, and that when he was finally sent to the SNY, he caught every cold and virus going around, because he hadn't been exposed to anyone else's germs for so long. His rap sheet was as thick as a legal reference book, but he'd become a mellow old-timer. Before he paroled, he showed me pictures of the grandchildren he would finally be on his way home to meet.

Trevor was in for ten years or so for molesting a young man. I should say, a younger man, because Trevor himself was a young man. He was one of the few clerks I had to fire. It seemed he had not really kicked his drug habit, and he was pilfering supplies from the library to trade for prescription painkillers from cunning inmates who had not swallowed their own. A conflicted gay man who'd been brought up in an ultra-religious home and had been closeted until he came to prison, Trevor also traded sexual favors for his necessary fix. Of course, I found out all of this later, after I'd hired and then had to fire him. I'd believed that he was clean and sober. I'd thought he was smart. I knew he was well read from all the books he'd checked out of the library before he worked there. I sympathized with how he'd never been able to be honest about his sexual orientation while he was growing up. If he ever got clean, he'd need therapy just for that. Only after he left did I realize that all the manic organizing he'd done of the legal forms, as well as the system he'd been in the process of creating for easier access to the resources of the law library, made no sense. It was as devoid of logic as an addict's mind. No one else could follow it.

Earl was a lifer in his fifties. Most people were scared of Earl and his time-tested mean scowl. He'd done hard time since he was a teenager but had asked to be transferred to the SNY for personal reasons: his mother was aged, and he felt it was high time to go home and take care of her. He well knew that a transfer to SNY indicated to the parole board that a lifer was earnestly trying to take advantage of rehabilitative programming in order to be deemed suitable for parole. Earl was fiercely loyal to me and to the library, to the point that he offered several times, *sotto voce*, to take a rude patron outside for me and teach him some manners. I suspected that he would have killed someone if I'd asked. I always thanked Earl for his thoughtfulness but assured him I could handle myself. I could do the job I was paid to do. (Also, I tried never to miss an opportunity to preach gender equity.) Earl was incarcerated because he had injured a man while he and his buddy were trying to steal the man's car in order to go to a concert: they had thrown the man in the trunk. Because this was technically kidnapping, he'd gotten a seven-year-to-life sentence. The fact that he was still in prison over thirty years later, though he'd been eligible for parole after just seven, showed that he did not play well with the parole board. Honest to a fault, Earl had no patience for pretense or mind-game-playing. His gruff and menacing manner fully camouflaged his good heart. The parole board eventually saw this, and he did get to go home.

Ramon was about the sweetest man I'd ever met. He and his brother were (literally) partners in crime and had received twin life sentences for a gang-related murder, but thanks to the capricious twists of an uneven justice system, his brother had already been released. Ramon's way of expressing himself was low-key. He usually only spoke after prompting, and I suspected his lack of the gift of gab had not served him well at parole board hearings. But nothing mean-spirited ever came from him. He was quietly generous to everyone. Ramon's book learning was limited, but he could fix anything. He totally understood the mechanics of how things worked. As these same mechanics are a mystery to me, I frequently relied on him for this skill. His Mexican name and appearance led me to assume he was bilingual, but his Spanish was not much better than mine. "I'm from Texas," he said, shrugging. "Even my mom says my Spanish is terrible." He had an infectious laugh, the kind of high-pitched giggle that is always surprising when it comes from a tough-looking guy with serious muscles. Ramon was one of my favorite people.

"Karma" was a nickname. When he first asked me to call him that—he assured me that I would not be able to pronounce his real Vietnamese name—I told him that I would not call him by anything that had been his gang moniker. But he said that his family had nicknamed him Karma, because he had survived the dreadful circumstances of being born aboard a boat of refugees fleeing Vietnam. He had joined a gang as an alienated teen and, of course, had broken the law. Specifically, he'd used a gun to help his homies rob a business and terrorize the customers. No one was hurt. He'd been sent to adult prison at the age of sixteen, something that, thank

God, we no longer do. Consequently, he had grown up fast and furious. Now in his thirties, Karma struggled with his anger. He could go from sunshine to full-on combat in the blink of an eye. But he also looked out for the less-able inmates, the ones who were mentally slow or weird or shunned, and who could be easily taken advantage of by other inmates. Karma was a gifted poet and visual artist. A prison journal even published some of his work. Hyperactive to the core, he redecorated the library with whatever supplies he could scrounge. I called him our own Martha Stewart, not because of the prison sentence, but because of his eye for color and style and flair. Ironically, even though he'd been born on a boat, when Karma was released, ICE promptly took him into custody, where he had to fight deportation to Vietnam, a country he'd never inhabited.

"Cuba" was also a nickname, referring to another young man's place of birth. Cuba was one of the original clerks in place when I started at the library, so he came with the job. At first I tried calling him by his actual given name, which was an uncommon one, but he didn't respond, and no one else knew whom I meant. So, Cuba it was. He was slow-moving and slow-talking. He actually seemed to know very little about the law, the area where he was stationed, but he was affable and well-liked by everyone. He'd been a youth offender who had "graduated" to an adult yard when he turned eighteen. Cuba was transferred to another facility not long after I started and has since been released. His commitment offense involved following along with the crowd more than any malevolence on his part, and I hope that, as an adult, he now hangs with a more law-abiding crowd.

I was going to say that Don had been a Marine, but according to Don, once a Marine, always a Marine, *semper fi*. Don had the crew cut and the tactical skills of a career military man. Don's coworkers didn't always appreciate his abrupt, snapping manner, but he got things done. (I was always surprised by the number of incarcerated veterans; they even had their own support group on the yard.) Don was instrumental in my ambitious plan to overhaul the physical layout of the library to make it more user-friendly. One administrator took an instant dislike to Don when she realized that I was relying on his spatial intelligence in this endeavor, as her mindset was that inmates were never to be trusted. She made unhelpful and frankly ignorant modifications to the proposed floor plan, just to show him who was in charge. (I noted over the years that the heavy-handed management style of several supervisors would befit the Hogwarts Grand Inquisitor.) We quietly went with Don's plan anyway. Don was going to have to register as a sex offender for the rest of his life because he had threatened a female acquaintance with rape while in a PTSD-induced blackout. He had come to his senses before committing the rape, but the attempt was enough to convince him to take a plea deal rather than risk a trial and perhaps a life sentence. He had kids. Don was one of the few inmates I observed who actively tried to parent his children from prison. He spoke to his wife and children on the phone as frequently as possible and kept apprised of their lives. Don didn't want his family to visit him for several reasons: he didn't want his kids to see him incarcerated, the trip was a long and expensive one, and his wife was undocumented. Don worried all the time that his wife would be deported and his kids would be placed in foster care, which was where he had grown up and which had been terribly damaging to him. Several times, he mailed his wife all the instructions and forms she needed to apply for US citizenship. I don't know if she ever successfully submitted them.

Billings. Ah, Billings. My first clue that maybe I shouldn't have hired Billings came when I asked one of the vocational instructors why she hadn't written him a recommendation for parole. "Because I fired him," she said. "He could *not* follow directions. And he's creepy." That gave me pause. When I hired him, he seemed like a good fit with the other clerks, and he was personable with our patrons. He was a fast learner. Maybe too fast. He read all the urban fiction books in our collection, which could be borderline pornographic, and when he discovered that I facilitated a weekly writers' group in the library, he thought he'd try his hand at writing some similarly provocative fiction. One afternoon, as the clerks were leaving for the day, Billings asked me to read the massive manuscript he'd written. After half a page, I realized that the sexy object of desire in this explicit first-person sexual fantasy was *me*. Granted, it was a younger, sultrier, far more suggestive version of me, but unmistakably me. Worse, it was unmistakably Billings as the narrator with an impressive erection. Yikes. I gave his handwritten tome to the disciplinary sergeant and fired Billings the next morning. I had to write him up for totally inappropriate behavior. "WHY would you think this was OK?" the sergeant reportedly asked him. "I thought she liked writing," Billings said, unfazed. He was sent to another yard, but for a few days, the officers had a little too much fun by subtly referring to some of the juicier passages in my presence. Dear reader, I did not keep a copy, so I can't quote word-for-word from Billings's purple prose.

Andres was a smooth talker, good-looking and articulate and persuasive. He was intelligent and picked up languages easily. He was an excellent interpreter and translator for the Spanish-speaking population on the yard. His four life sentences for gang-related murders were intended to run long after his natural death, but recent changes in the law with regard to the decision-making capabilities of adolescent offenders offered him a glimmer of hope for release someday. I discovered after I'd hired him that Andres was a rather careless worker—he'd cross off books as returned when they had not been, or he'd shelve the returns haphazardly—but he had charisma. Along with his ease with languages, he had a dead-on ear for dialogue: as a member of the writers' group, he was working on a horror novel that was formulaic, but the dialogue he'd written sparkled with authenticity and wit. I encouraged him to turn it into a screenplay. He was a natural.

Caleb had been a high school teacher. It was a good bet that a middle-aged white guy with no tattoos who was housed on an SNY was in for some kind of sex crime, and Caleb fit the profile. He had molested a teenage girl who babysat his children. As a result of his conviction, he'd lost career and marriage and family. I didn't think he was a serial predator, but I also knew that just because this had been his only arrest didn't mean he hadn't taken advantage of his position of authority and abused other young women he'd been responsible to educate. I met him when he was a clerk for the Catholic chaplain and hired him when he had termed out of that job; inmates were only allowed to keep a job for two years, in order to discourage over-familiarity with staff. Caleb was extremely organized, almost obsessively devoted to detail, and he whipped the legal area into shape after Trevor had left behind that aforementioned unfinished and nonsensical filing system. I trusted the integrity of his work and wrote him a letter of recommendation upon his release.

Eduardo was an unassuming, quiet, short man, and he put up with every short joke on the yard with good humor. Eduardo had participated in a gang-related murder and was serving a life sentence. Like so many inmates, he would be deported if he were ever found suitable for parole. He hadn't lived in Mexico since he was a little boy, but family members in Mexico were prepared to take him in, to give him a place to live and provide him with a job. Eduardo was bilingual after so many years in the US, but he still struggled to pass his GED. He had actually passed the language part, but he'd failed the math part a couple of times. Many years after the fact, he realized that he had started skipping school and getting into trouble because he had an undiagnosed learning disability and, like many teenagers, would rather have been known as a troublemaker than as dumb. Eduardo was a living example of the generational cycle of prison: one of his nephews was now incarcerated. His nephew wanted to believe that Eduardo was still a bad-ass convict whom he wanted to imitate. He didn't want to hear that Eduardo had decided to change his ways and become a model prisoner after his father had died and he hadn't been able to attend the funeral or comfort his mother. His nephew saw the old Eduardo as a role model and scoffed at the new, improved Eduardo, which hurt Eduardo's heart. He wanted to save his nephew from the many wasted years of pain and bad decisions in prison that he himself had known. His sister, the nephew's mother, begged Eduardo over the phone to do whatever he could to straighten her son out, but his nephew wouldn't listen to him. "Welcome to the world of parenting," I told him.

These character sketches represent many library clerks with whom I worked. Clerks came and went over the years, often with little notice of their departure. They could be transferred to another facility or unexpectedly released on parole or reassigned to a vocational or educational program. The library was not considered a priority job, even though I sometimes fought with the Inmate Assignments office to keep a good worker employed there. I usually lost the argument.

The library clerks had to walk a fine line between being an inmate and doing their jobs. They had to use their people skills. They had to be tactful and professional, on time and well groomed. Displeased patrons sometimes accused them of "wearing green," an insult meaning that they were acting like correctional cops instead of like inmates wearing blue. The clerks were tasked with applying the library rules to everyone, which didn't always go over well with their friends, who perhaps expected preferential treatment or sketchy favors.

During those first days, my scant official training left me in a position of having to rely on the clerks to teach me the ways of the library. Which meant that my BS monitor had to be fully charged. I had high expectations for my clerks, but I knew they weren't always saints.

I owe much of my legal education to Inmate Cummings, a desiccated string bean of an old man who was the most litigious inmate on the yard. Cummings realized within my first days in the library that I had no legal background. Rather than treat my ignorance dismissively, which I'm pretty sure would have been his go-to behavior, Cummings decided to be magnanimous and show me the ropes. He explained to me things like the hierarchy of state and federal courts and how to obtain the proper forms for each court and how many copies of a motion each court required and the complicated process of filing an appeal and following it to its natural end. He would have made a good teacher in another life. Cummings predicted that someday, as a result of his stellar and unceasing work on his case, inmates in the future would cite *in re Cummings* as a precedent. This was not to be. Some months later, bonier and frailer, Cummings was transferred to a medical facility. I was genuinely saddened when he died of cancer.

Back to the physical library. My office was a room carved from the library's expanse. Its walls were made of windows from waist-level up to ceiling, so I could see everything going on in the library. Even the door was half window, contributing to the fishbowl feel of my work setting. Fortunately, the window into the inmate restroom just behind my office was painted opaquely about halfway up, sparing me an inadvertent look at any intimate details. The blind spots out on the floor among the shelves were made visible by those parabolic mirrors you see on blind curves on country roads.

My office door locked, so that my computer and phone and files—and my person—could be secure in any time of upheaval. I'd been instructed to lock it any time I was not in it, even if only for a moment. My office was considered a "red zone," which meant it was a no-go for inmates: the words "OUT OF BOUNDS" were painted right onto the floor outside my door, as well as on the approach to any other areas of the library that were off limits to patrons. The library clerks could only enter my office with my permission. Ensconced there, I was like a dictator of a small country: my word was final.

Although those of us who worked within the confines of a yard, rather than in an area outside of a secure yard perimeter, were not permitted to bring personal items into our workspaces, I found ways to de-institutionalize my office. I scrounged around for posters from the education department and taped them to the faded walls. I smuggled in seasonal decorations. Karma painted the trim around the windows a murky lavender; Lord only knows where he got the paint and brush. He stenciled hearts onto my metal trashcan, then asked me not to tell anyone that he had been the artist. As though no one knew.

Outside of my office, we plastered the bulletin boards with colored paper, on which we rotated news clippings or other interesting items. We posted a "Quote of the Day," a "Word of the Day," and a "Book of the Day." I printed out NPR's *Weekend Edition* weekly puzzle and awarded a star-sticker to whoever solved it first—glimmers of normal fun in the library.

Sometimes my office hosted night visitors, first watch officers who left evidence of their presence. My phone might be moved, or there might be boot prints where on-duty slackers had propped their feet against the desk. There might be sticky coffee cup rings or crumbs of food. I imagined the empty library was a tempting place for an officer to steal some sleep on an overnight shift. Occasionally, my computer showed signs of use. Rarely, my office door was left unlocked. For some reason, on several three-day weekends, someone used the urinal in the inmate bathroom and did not flush it, leaving a sour pee smell to greet me on my morning back. I complained to the sergeant, but since my daytime shift was during second watch, he wasn't the sergeant for the wee-hours (pun intended) first watch, so he didn't much care. I also complained when parts of my "WELCOME" sign just inside the main door were strategically erased one night to read "WE CUM." Seriously? They might be highly compensated correctional officers, but some of them reveled in a frat-boy culture.

These untidy transgressions were even more noticeable because my office usually sparkled with spotlessness. When I hired Earl, he made himself the chief deputy of cleaning my office. The first time he stripped and waxed and buffed the linoleum floor in my office, we discovered that its actual color was closer to lime green than olive. My floor gleamed like a miniature ballroom dance floor in the middle of a prison. It was so beautiful that I felt badly when my shoes made scuff marks. Earl insisted on waxing it every week.

I was often struck by how meticulous about cleanliness and hygiene most of my clerks were. Because they had so little to call their own, they were extremely careful with and protective of what was theirs. They also had so little personal space that it was important to keep it in order. Plus, when you had little control over your life and the minutes and hours of your day, maybe you were hyper-super-predisposed to control anything you could. Anyway, the library and my office were kept much more spic-and-span than my house was. Compared to these men, I was sloppy about my office and my stuff. I was glad they couldn't see my home. I have too much stuff even to catalog.

With experience, I felt at home in the library. The busy days flew, and in no time flat I felt like a fixture. Some days I suspected that I could be replaced by a robot that could use a copy machine, but other days I felt that one irreplaceable thing I brought to the library was humanity. Really, I was part mom, part cheerleader, and part walking dictionary, but most of all I was a human, interacting with other humans. This should not have been rare in prison, but apparently it was.

People used to ask me if I was scared to work so closely with inmates. I wasn't. I joked that it was more like working at a day care center. They may be grown men, but they have so many questions! So many needs! So little patience! But these inmate coworkers were my work family. The library was a sunny spot in the prison, a place of information and learning, a community of human beings being determinedly human.

And for me there was more—the breath of the Holy Spirit in my face as I sometimes looked down the rows of regulars, each one unique and baffling and sometimes aggravating, concentrating on their tasks, sitting on their unyielding orange chairs, daylight streaming through those high windows, faces absorbed by their stacks of handwritten motions and appeals, and I felt a love that can only come from God.

Library Work

For book lovers, a good library is one of the exquisite pleasures of this life. Libraries may lack the new-book smell of a fancy bookstore, but they exude an aura of ancient wisdom, a whiff of timelessness. Each volume in a library, be it a classic tome or a trashy novel, bears a legacy of a long list of previous readers. The mission of a library is to preserve history as well as to circulate the new, stitching past to present with an eye toward posterity.

The library as a repository of knowledge is as old as civilization. Some five thousand years ago, a library in Mesopotamia held thirty thousand clay tablets. The most famous ancient library, the Great Library of Alexandria in Egypt, was said to feature nearly 750,000 scrolls made of papyrus or leather. This was not a public library: access to the painstakingly hand-copied scrolls was restricted to scholars with literary qualifications. But it made Alexandria an intellectual capital of its time. The Roman Empire was home to at least three libraries that were available to teachers and scholars. By the third century AD, regular folks could look at books, oddly enough, at the public baths.

The spread of Christianity and early monasticism were instrumental in preserving libraries and the art of the written word through the Dark Ages. The dawn of the Renaissance saw a return to the Greek and Roman classics for inspiration, as well as the establishment of universities with libraries. Gutenberg's movable-type printing press in the 1400s replaced handwritten manuscripts with printed books, sparking the creation of many national libraries throughout Europe. The oldest library in the United States began with a donation of four hundred books by a clergyman named John Harvard to a new university in Massachusetts, an institution that eventually bore his name. Ben Franklin opened a subscription library in Philadelphia, wherein membership dues purchased books that could then be borrowed for free. When the US Library of Congress was burned to ashes by the British during the War of 1812, the federal government bought Thomas Jefferson's extensive private collection and rebuilt from there. The first public library in America opened in New Hampshire in 1833, and the idea of public libraries spread nationally along with the philosophy of free public education for children.

Public libraries appeal to the citizen in me. A public library, by definition, welcomes all the public. It's a community service, not unlike K-12 schools or road maintenance or public safety institutions, provided for the common good by the taxes we pay. There are rules for using the public library, but there is no entrance fee, no purchase requirement, no exclusive membership clause, making the library an equal-opportunity refuge.

More recently, public libraries provide access to technology for people who may not be able to afford personal devices that give entrance to the online world. The resources available at a public library today go beyond the printed word, allowing everyone a chance to touch the wonders of the digital age and to use the internet for research or social networking.

I have known a few germophobic people who never visit the public library, citing the risk of contamination from public spaces and from books handled by others. No amount of scented hand sanitizer would make them feel safe in such a setting. When I borrow books, however, I feel virtuous. I feel like I am saving money, consuming fewer raw materials, and making good use of my tax dollars.

Having spent many happy hours in libraries in schools, universities, and various cities, the years I got to work in one delighted me. Since my library was in a prison, I found that every day was a new opportunity for learning. I got to spend my working hours among books and people who liked books—or who at least were seeking brief respite in a sometimes tense environment. I thought of how, all my life, teachers, counselors, and parents advised, "Find something you love to do, and then get somebody to pay you to do it." How cool that, at a ripe age, I'd finally landed in that job.

Used Books

Browsing a second-hand bookstore offers hours of pleasure to book lovers like me. Every city has its dusty corners of used books, places that act like a drug on us book addicts. I even like the book sections in thrift stores like the Salvation Army or Goodwill. The variety of volumes that end up on the fifty-cent shelf always amazes me.

I often imagine the circumstances that led to the donation of particular books to second-hand stores: death, divorce, downsizing. Someday the piles of books in my house may meet the same fate, leading future readers to ponder what kind of person previously owned or read this or that volume.

Books that once belonged to others have a different character from the brand new books in bookstores, with their uncracked spines and freshly minted smell. A well-used book has that aura of having been enjoyed and even loved, which gives it a personality. Sometimes the previous owners of books leave behind traces of their lives, clues to their identity: a bookmark or a letter, a ticket stub or a grocery list, or (rarely) actual money. These bits and pieces of a life only add to the book's mystique.

My prison library was full of weird and wonderful old books, spanning decades of lending and borrowing. We had books on topics such as the urgent situation of the Cold War with the USSR and a mathematical discipline called Seven Place Natural Trigonometrical Functions. One outdated medical tome gave advice on the number of cigarettes a pregnant woman should ideally smoke in a day. A few volumes dated back into the 1890s. We periodically culled from the shelves the ones in disrepair or the ones that no one had checked out since the 1970s. But I just couldn't throw away some of the antiquated gems, and so a little museum took over a shelf in my office.

The inscriptions in some of our old books, mysterious sentiments that made sense to the writer and recipient, left us wondering about these ghosts. "To Mother, for your birthday, from Jim," said a 1925 copy of *Mrs. Dalloway* by Virginia Woolf. Perhaps Mother was a feminist. And this inscription in a volume of the *Chicken Soup* franchise, signed by Dan and Sharon: "Thanks for everything you've done for the team!" Only our imaginations could fill in what team and what was done. A weathered book called *2nd Course in Algebra*, published in 1911, belonged to a student named George Russell. Folded into the back of the book was an instructor's pamphlet containing the answers, which made me wonder if young George and his cheater's heart had ended up doing any time himself.

Sometimes it seems that books are on their way to obsolescence. We live in an increasingly bookless world, where information and entertainment are digital and intangible. Even libraries are modernizing, becoming sleek repositories of computers and technology. Maybe that's why I was so content in my dinosaur library, with its relics and throwbacks. An old book looks like history, smells like memory, feels like treasure from the past. The cover, the binding, the color and weight of the paper, the typeset, the quaintness of the illustrations—all of these details evoke a reverent wistfulness in my heart. I suspect that future generations will not feel the same sweet nostalgia when they come across an old Kindle. Then again, maybe they will.

Overdue

Winner of the most ironic overdue notice sent from my library: "The book you checked out from the Facility D Library, entitled 'Personal Responsibility,' is now thirty days overdue."

In most libraries, an overdue book is not a major deal. Patrons might have their borrowing privileges curtailed until the book is returned, owe a fine, or even pay to replace the lost volume. The first time I sent out overdue notices through the institutional mail for my library, however, the consequences were unforeseen (by me) and immediate. Inmates who had not returned their books in a timely manner were called into the sergeant's office, verbally reprimanded for causing trouble in the library, and then subjected to a locker search. Locker searches are brutal because, depending on who is conducting them, an inmate might find all of his belongings flung around his bunk and covered in the remnants of his precious food supply. This can mean hot sauce stuck on photos, instant coffee wetly staining legal papers, books ripped apart, stationery ruined, clothing soiled, snacks no longer edible, a soggy mess of intentional destruction. And, for good measure, the lockers of the men living on either side of the targeted inmate also get hit, so the guy who messed up is left with nothing but a bunk full of chaos and the simmering resentment of his dorm neighbors.

After that spate of incidents, which I heard about in living color the next day, I changed our policy. Rather than mailing them, I gave the overdue notices to Earl to deliver in person, quietly, under the disciplinary radar. Earl apparently delivered these notices with such a threatening countenance that the books he sought surfaced almost immediately. Earl enjoyed putting the fear of God into disrespectful book borrowers. He would have been a success in a collections department.

The overdue notices taught me, once again, that the things I considered no big deal could be a huge deal in prison. I couldn't bring in hand sanitizer, because the alcohol content made it an attractive drink. I couldn't pack my lunch of leftovers in a glass dish, because broken glass can cut things, like throats. I couldn't display family photos on my desk, as those dear faces might beckon to stalkers. I couldn't forget to stow my cell phone in my car, because a staff member caught with a cell phone on the yard could be charged with a misdemeanor and lose a percentage of pay. I couldn't wear anything blue, or I might be mistaken for an inmate during an incident. And I learned time and again that the biggest deal of all in prison was "respect."

In prison, respect is the coin of the realm. The library ran smoothly when it ran on mutual respect. I was a pretty good boss, but the bar is low in prison: one of my clerks told me that he liked working in the library because "you treat us like people." Treating people like people seems like a no-brainer to me, but that is the essence of respect.

Respect is all that is left when a person's dignity is methodically stripped down to nothing. An inmate has no personal space, no privacy, no power, no voice in anything that happens to him, but he can command and give respect. If any word or deed is tinged with the slightest "disrespect," all hell could break loose. Many dialogues start with, "No disrespect, but . . ."

The literal meaning of "respect" is "to take a second look." Every word in prison is second-guessed, mulled over, dissected. This is possibly due to the fact that people have a lot of free time when they are incarcerated. With a surfeit of time, mole-hills can become mountains. Respect is universally desired; disrespect is hunted, ferreted out. Sometimes I caught a thieving patron hiding a magazine in his pocket or trying to smuggle a book out of the library, a blatant act of disrespect that, for my own credibility, I had to write up as a rules infraction. "Bunch of crooks around here," I'd mutter to my clerks, which made them laugh, but they knew: Disrespect must not stand.

Mailing the overdue notices was disrespectful on my part, but keeping a book past its due date was disrespecting the library. In prison-think, I guessed we were even.

The Letter R

In 2005, the state department I worked for, known as the CDC, had the letter *R* added to its acronym, making it the California Department of Corrections and Rehabilitation. This fancy name came compliments of Governor Arnold Schwarzenegger. It also heralded a change in penal attitude, but attitudes change very slowly.

In my experience, the *R* of CDCR could also stand for ridicule. Sometimes the newly added letter was written in lower case, as though the concept of rehabilitation was not to be dignified with a capital letter. Sometimes the *R* was even scratched off official signs by cynical employees. The idea of a criminal being rehabilitated was a joke to many of my co-workers, who considered inmates a less-than-human breed, and who found it easy to demonize those they did not care to know. To some, the letter *R* also signified recidivism, as the clerical workers in Records processed the same offenders over and over, men who did their time and then came back through the prison's revolving door as parole violators. The system was long overdue for an overhaul.

I believed that rehabilitation was our most important task in affecting the daily life of an inmate. A term in prison had the potential to be a life-altering, slap-in-the-face event, if those incarcerated were given the tools to succeed when they were back on the outside. I believed in the practical things like GEDs, job training, money management, anger management, and treatment for addictions, of course, but I believed true rehabilitation came from the epiphany that, as a child of God, you were loved and forgiven. It was almost a prison cliché that inmates found Jesus behind bars, but I knew so many men who looked deep into their own hearts and were quite sure that they could never be forgiven, not even by God. They had no faith in themselves, and they realized that the families they had abandoned or let down had little faith in them, too. They were in a bad place, both geographically and spiritually.

I believed that people who thought they were broken could be fixed. With care, a shift in priorities, and proper funding, the *R* could be the biggest letter in our department's acronym. I believed that human dignity could overcome human failing, if only given a fighting chance. During my years working in the prison, I saw many men pick up the pieces of broken lives and fit them carefully back together. The seams showed, but they held.

I was privileged to see the letter *R* come to life in our library, in the men who participated in self-help programs, who sincerely worked on changing their behavior, and who reached out to be of service both to their fellow inmates and their families. The power of the letter *R* resided in the stories of the men who left and did not come back. The lifers who earned release dates, under the system's new appreciation for the letter *R* and thanks to the corresponding shift in the Parole Board commissioners' mentality, were especially inspirational, as their recidivism rate was practically nil. I used to tell them before they paroled that I hoped I'd never see them again, at least not in prison. They were the personification of hope. They had prepared themselves for the potential day of release, another *R* word. They'd been deemed suitable to rejoin society. They faced a difficult transition to life on the outside, but they demonstrated that the letter *R* could save lives.

After I retired (my own *R* word), I met with some of the men from the library. How surreal and yet perfectly comfortable it was to have a cup of coffee with a former inmate who was really an old friend. The men struggled to adjust to the outside, to find work, to secure housing, to make friends, to go on a date, to use a cell phone, to navigate a changed society, but in their view, the struggle was all good. Of course they had their demons, just as we all do. But they had been to hell and back. Now they were on a joyful road. They were free, brought to them by the letter *R*.

Precious and Precarious

"If this is the way you will deal with me, then please do me the favor of killing me at once, so that I need no longer face this distress."
—Moses, to God (Numbers 11:15)

In the prison library, the news still arrived the old-fashioned way, meaning in print, not online. Among the inmates who frequented the library, current events were discussed at length. During one week, the news had been full of death. There were the reports of a couple of famous musicians taking their own lives, which, although they were strangers, made the library patrons feel as though they'd lost someone they knew and loved personally. There was the teenage girl coaxing her boyfriend via persistent text messages to commit suicide, which he tragically did. There was a feature story in the newspaper about a man with terminal cancer who had availed himself of California's new End of Life Option Act law, intentionally taking a prescribed lethal dose of medication.

One of my patrons that week, mystified by the suicides of people who seemed to have a great life going, posed a simple question.

"Do people out there not want to live?" he asked.

People out there. Free people, he meant. People who can do just about anything they please. People not doing time in a state prison, cut off from society's company and progress. People like me and my family and everyone I knew.

Do we not want to live?

The question lingered in my mind. It came from a man who knows what it is to take a life. Serving a life sentence for murder, he also knew what it was to lose the meaningful parts of a life out there: freedom, family, career, marriage, mobility, variety, personal space, personal safety. Things I take for granted, the small pleasures and the deeply gratifying moments and even the daily irritants, were the stuff of impossible dreams for him.

God's gift of life, so precious and so precarious, was the topic that day. Through the grace of God, we humans can give life, but we can also end it. It cannot be restored once it is taken from another, no matter how real the killer's remorse. Yet we can become blasé about, and even unaware of, the miracle of each lived day of our lives. The incessant bad news can inoculate us against feeling anything about the death that invades and conquers life, through war, through terrorism, through crime, through neglect, through disasters, through accidents, through suicides. We become too numb even to mourn its loss.

Maybe sometimes out here we don't want to live, when we lose hope, when we suffer from depression, when we don't see any future. We are tired. We understand the allure of just giving up. We can feel like Moses in the desert, crying out to an angry God: *Just end it already!* But it's not only people out here who fall into despair. Suicide is a dark and seductive companion in prison as well. People who are incarcerated often feel abandoned, shunned, vilified as less than human. They suspect that they are the throwaway members of society, whose lives matter less than others'. Sometimes those of us who work in prisons are guilty of confirming that suspicion.

My library lifer could not imagine a free person not reveling in freedom, not treasuring the privilege of such a life. I could not imagine being locked up for life and still carrying on with dignity and purpose, as many lifers do. This is why it was good for us to talk. I finally answered him that we mostly do want to live out here. It's just that sometimes we forget to be grateful for the gift.

The Grace of Acceptance

Prison is not the place I ever expected to learn anything about God. But I did. The God of Surprises was always evident in my workplace, gently reminding me that every person, no matter how guilty, is a gifted and beloved child of our God.

Among the inmates who turned up in the library were wildly talented artists and writers, musicians and mathematicians. There were chefs who could make magic out of ramen and repairmen who could fix anything. There were remarkable innovators and some of the most ecologically minded people I've known.

Most impressive, however, was the serenity among the men who engaged in a program of self-improvement. I was always amazed by the lack of bitterness, among some of those I worked with, in response to a major disappointment. Since I am bitter when my newspaper isn't in my driveway on time—my morning is *ruined*!—I was often stunned by the purity of their acceptance. Like the clerk whose lawyer told him that if he'd had better representation way back when, he could have been out of prison ten years ago.

"You could have been free ten years ago?" I said. "Doesn't that upset you?"

He shrugged. "I guess I had things to learn still," he said.

Or the lifer whose bid for release was rejected by the parole board; told that, even after decades of self-help work, he was not ready to rejoin society. In my dealings with him, he was a decent, compassionate person, so I was bitter on his behalf. Surely the board had made a mistake.

"No, they were fair," he said. "They're doing their job."

He would have the chance to go before the board again. He would strive anew to show that he was truly rehabilitated. I watched him submit to the authorities over him and move forward with quiet integrity.

Such a lesson in grace: the grace of acceptance.

Because even as these men were paying some serious debts to society, they were examples of how to work with the concrete reality of *what is.* They didn't protest. They weren't resentful of circumstances out of their control, when board hearings were delayed, when visits were cancelled, when the yard was locked down. They rolled with the punches; they played the hands they were dealt; they danced, as the old saying goes, with the ones that brung them. All things that I was not at all good at doing.

I saw up close some inspiring and heartbreaking examples of the grace of letting go. Sometimes an inmate had to say goodbye quickly to a friend because of a transfer. Close friendships are hard to come by in prison, where inmates are always on guard against each other, against being taken advantage of, against getting played for a fool. Maybe they are protecting themselves from the feeling of loss when a friend departs, or maybe they are too used to loss. But deep friendships still form, and then good buddies must say goodbye with no real expectation of ever seeing each other again. They are sad, but with an admirable lack of self-pity, they let it go. It's just another rotten part of being in prison. I can only pray to approximate this grace of acceptance in my life.

It may seem that I am glorifying people who were incarcerated. And maybe I am. Maybe they acquiesced because they didn't dare to dream, because they had been shot down, figuratively and sometimes literally, so many times. There was so much brokenness in prison. But there was also authentic kindness and brotherly love and grace and God. Acceptance, I saw, is a function of mindfulness. It is a learned skill, but it reminds us that our God is ever in charge, both in and out of prison.

No In-Between

The inmates housed on the medium security yard seemed to be either very young—like fresh-out-of-high-school young—or elderly. Like, old men. Those who actually were middle-aged usually passed for old men, due to the complications of substance abuse and poor self-care. I really noticed the aged population, and was a little shocked by it, when the "Wish List" I posted for new library books filled with requests for medical reference books. And not just on any medical issues, but old-age things like prostate problems, arthritis, and hip replacements. The young men were the fighters, full of piss and vinegar, out for revenge anytime one felt disrespected, which could mean anything from an actual physical altercation to messing with another man's belongings to an untoward and unlucky glance. Disrespect was a sin just above snitching.

In contrast, my older clerks were careful to avoid all drama. They counted their disciplinary-free time in years. "Last time I was in a fight," Earl told me, "my hands hurt for two weeks." He shook his head at the memory.

The young inmates had two main requests on the Wish List: anime books and urban fiction. Anime, in case you need some clarification, as I did, is a Japanese stylized cartoon book that you read from back to front. The anime books come in a never-ending series and seem to be addictive. Urban fiction is an American stylized soft porn, like if Sidney Sheldon wrote from the 'hood. These also come in series and seem to be addictive. Inmates of all ages devoured any books of the "true crime" genre that detailed misdeeds both historical and current. Maybe they were comparing notes.

The old inmates had either been incarcerated for decades or had been in and out of prison their entire adult lives. They were mostly over it. "Let's face it," Earl said, "we're proof that you can teach an old dog new tricks." Once they wised up to the situation, they were committed to getting out and never coming back. The young ones still thought that they were different from the old guys. They didn't yet see their future selves in the weathered faces of the elderly. They thought they were too smart to be stuck in the prison cycle like these old guys. And of course they weren't. Every now and then, though, a younger inmate would be talking to an older inmate and I could see the realization dawning in the younger man's face that if he didn't get his act together, he was looking at himself in twenty or thirty years. Lessons lurked in every corner of prison, waiting to be learned.

One day, a pleasant, older inmate named McClive sauntered into the library while a couple of younger inmates were checking out their books.

"It's my Saturday," announced McClive. "I'm off today. I already walked the dog and washed the car. The wife and kids are off somewhere. I'm gonna watch the game and take an old-man nap."

The young inmates looked at him like he was crazy. "Old fool," muttered one, as McClive tipped an imaginary hat and left the building.

But I got it. How else could a man endure the ache of the complete loss of these ordinary things we take for granted, especially if he were old enough to understand all that he'd lost? Maybe a Saturday afternoon in fantasy helped. I know that moment with McClive made me appreciate my ordinary Saturdays a little more.

Psych Reports

If a lifer came into the library clean-shaven and carefully pressed and seemed a little nervous, but it was not a visiting day, I knew what day it was. "Psych eval today," he'd mention a little too casually. "Just waiting for them to call me."

The report that came from the psych eval, or psychiatric evaluation, was one of the most important documents that the Parole Board considered when deciding if an inmate serving a life term was suitable for parole. The prison psychologist was in charge of making a determination of the risk factor in releasing an inmate back into society. Lifers prayed for a "LOW" verdict. "LOW-TO-MODERATE" might work, but

"MODERATE" pretty much meant that you were not getting out anytime soon. The psychologist took into account the past, meaning the family history and childhood, the crime that led to incarceration, and the behavior while in prison; the present, meaning how the guy presented himself in the face-to-face interview and whether he was "programming" (taking advantage of all educational and self-help opportunities on the yard) and staying disciplinary-free; and the future, meaning how was he likely to fare on the outside and if he was likely to reoffend or pose any danger to society. So the psych eval was a combination of history, observation, and crystal ball. It carried a ton of weight.

Inmates could request a new psych eval after a certain number of years, or they could go with the old one, especially if it was a "LOW" or if the psychologist was pressed for time. Inmates also shared their knowledge of which psychologists were harder or softer in their evaluations. One might be known as a pushover, for example, while another might be pegged as a man-hater. You got who you got, however; your future could depend on the luck of the draw. Many inmates felt that the final psych report showed them in a far less flattering light than they thought they'd presented themselves. But even though most often psychologists based the entire report on one interview and a close perusal of the inmate's paper trail, they mostly were not dumb or born yesterday.

The psych eval and report were done several months before the hearing date, and the inmate received a copy of the report before the hearing. Lifers dissected and analyzed these reports meticulously, deciphering the psych-lingo, reading deep meaning into single words, citing other words as code, and above all, drawing cautionary observations that could benefit themselves and others in future interviews.

The lifers on my yard ran a support group that aimed to help each other navigate their parole hearings successfully. They were generous with their time and their own experiences. They held mock parole board hearings for the guys going to a hearing for the first time. Some delighted in playing the role of the tough parole board commissioner. They'd offer conflicting advice: Don't be too shy. But don't be too overconfident. Don't be too happy. But don't be too contrite. Be real. Be yourself. But don't overdo the sincerity thing.

The lifers were like an exclusive club you didn't really want to join, as none of the members had any guarantee of being released. They celebrated when one got a date and commiserated when another was denied. They also closely analyzed the transcripts of each other's parole board hearings, which each inmate received a month or so after the fact.

I was always impressed by the grace that inmates displayed in the face of both success and failure at the board. They faced their past and atoned for their crimes and planned for an uncertain future, all while trying to present themselves honestly. The outcome was either a release date or a return to self-reflection and self-help. I tried to imagine the stress of facing both the prison psychologist and the board commissioners, and I knew that I would be a quaking, blathering bundle of nerves at either meeting. I was ready to wet my pants at every mundane job interview I'd ever endured. If my freedom were at stake, I'd fold up like origami. I'd never get out.

One afternoon, a distraught lifer came into the library to report that he'd been called to his psych eval that morning with *no advance notice*. He hadn't ironed his best shirt, he hadn't shaved, and he hadn't had time to prep himself mentally. He knew he'd done badly, and he felt it was a nefarious plot by the prison administration to assure that he'd get a "MODERATE" at best. Since he sued the warden about once a week, I thought perhaps his conspiracy theory was not that far-fetched.

An unfavorable psych report was one of the worst things that could happen to a lifer. But even if the psychologists only

spent a few hours with each inmate being evaluated, they usually got it right. That was their job.

Sex Offenders and Me: An Uneasy Alliance

Although I had worked in the Records Office and could access the contents of every inmate's Central File, I tended not to look up the commitment offenses of the inmates on my yard. I wanted to see the library patrons as people first, and convicts by the way. Obviously, they were incarcerated for a reason, but that reason did not need to color my professional interaction with them. The only files I consulted were those of the prospective clerks I was thinking of hiring. But I knew that a Sensitive Needs Yard housed those most unsavory and despicable of criminals, the sex offenders.

Some staff members refused to hire any inmate convicted of a sex crime, but that was an awfully big slice of the SNY population. One clerical worker I knew had rather hired a guy who had shot up his high school and killed people than a child molester. My main criteria for employment were someone who was honest, who was helpful, and with whom my other clerks could work without drama. The final decision was mine, but I took the suggestions of the clerks seriously in my search for an employee who would be agreeable to all.

A new hire also had to have completed his GED; those with-out were liable to be yanked out of the library job and into a classroom without notice. That had happened with Eduardo: one minute he was a library clerk, and the next he was told to report to the GED prep class, where he had to stay until he passed every part of the test. Having to hire and train a new clerk on little notice slowed down the pleasant chugging along of the library machine. Those of us who supervised groups of inmates were supposed to hire them in a way that reflected the ethnic make-up of the yard, which was sorted into the categories of White, Black, Hispanic, or Other. I also tried to have at least one bilingual clerk, if not two, because a significant percentage of our patrons were primarily Spanish-speakers.

Over the years, I hired several convicted child molesters and one rapist. Will had broken into a neighboring woman's apartment and raped her repeatedly over the course of a whole, long, nightmarish night. He'd been a teenager in an alcohol-induced blackout, but he owned his crime and was serving a life sentence with a possibility of parole in twenty years. It was hard to picture Will doing such terrible things to his victim. When I hired him, he told me in his humble manner the circumstances of his crime and said he understood if I didn't want to work with him. I'd known him from my time as a self-help group sponsor, and he was active in various self-help groups on the yard. Will had quietly organized an unofficial support group for several other sex offender registrants, men who were remorseful and wanted to rehabilitate themselves in a meaningful way, but who feared the stigma of attending such a group openly. He had asked me to look up some resources for the group, but to keep it confidential.

Will was the one who made me question my own preconceptions. As a survivor of a sexually abusive male babysitter when I was little and a male teacher in high school, I knew the damage that sex offenders caused their victims. Victims often spend a lifetime trying to make peace with, or at least get past, the trauma they experienced at the hands of someone just like Will. As the mother of daughters, I knew my own murderous reaction to the thought of my girls suffering any such abuse.

But now I knew Will as a person. Even though I had read the police report detailing the unspeakable things he'd done to his victim, I knew him to be kind and sincere and generous to others. He had grown up in prison and was definitely not the young man who had come into prison years ago. My heart saw God in him. But my brain rebelled at the thought of giving him a pass on what he'd done to the woman who still lived with the cruel reality of her victimization. What kind of woman and mother was I, to befriend this monster?

And maybe that is where God comes in, to help us hold conflicting thoughts within us and not surrender to either. Maybe that is where God's grace is most present to us. No matter what Will had done, no matter how the rest of us might judge him and condemn him, he would always be a beloved child of God. That didn't mean I had to like him (or any other inmate who had done something heinous), but it did mean that I could appreciate his journey from that crime to the person he was now. And most importantly, that I could support his recovery and rehabilitation even when society might not.

Like the staff member who opted to hire the murderer over a sex offender, society does not forgive. This is manifested in the lifetime registration requirement for sex offenders. Anyone convicted of a sex offense in California must register annually with their local law enforcement agency and must promptly update any address changes. This information is public. A convicted sex offender will thus face some difficult challenges in securing housing, employment, or even a friend, much less a date.

I am not saying that all convicted sex offenders are harmless once they are released from prison. Some offenders should definitely never be released. Some who are released will never be rehabilitated and do bear close watching to guard against their opportunity to reoffend. But I am saying that, just like every person, every case is unique. Also, there are degrees of sex offenses that are not reflected on the registry. The most extreme example I met was an inmate who returned to prison because he had failed to register in a timely manner, but whose only conviction for a sex offense was for public urination. A drunk peeing behind a bar is gross, but he's not a sex offender. Another inmate, who was also a library clerk, had had to register for life because he'd had consensual sex with his sixteen-year-old girlfriend when he was eighteen. He had later married her and had children with her. They lived a normal life until the registry went public. Once his name and address were available online, he was driven from his neighborhood, had to change his phone number, and lost his job. He then developed a drug habit that cost him his family and his freedom. He had major problems, obviously, but he was hardly a dangerous or serial sex offender. I agree with the current push to update and refine these lifelong registration requirements, so that they more accurately reflect the actual danger to the public.

Then there was Will. He really was a rapist. If he was released from prison, he'd have to register as a sex offender for life. This was the law. It was also going to complicate his every attempt to be a productive member of society. Although he will have served his time and paid his debt, society's rules were going to dog him and label him forever. Will accepted this. He believed he deserved this fate. But knowing him sure made me ponder the true nature of justice, mercy, and forgiveness. How do you befriend a rapist and still look your daughters in the eye? I'm still working on that. It's an uneasy place to be. It's also a ripe example of the mystery of God's grace.

Visits with Brothers

"I was in prison, and you visited me."
—Matthew 25:36

"Jesus Is My Homeboy"
—T-shirt randomly spotted

When my husband and I moved to the small town where he had taken a teaching job, we'd been married for five years, had two children (with two still to come), and felt like old hands at life, which, in retrospect, we were not. As we adjusted to village life, we soon learned that our new home's main industry was a state prison. Coming from the diverse metropolis of Los Angeles, this seemed to us like another planet. The prison facility squatted, ominous and foreboding, where a two-lane highway out of town dead-ended. Even though we met many people who worked there, we never went near it.

But that was before we became detention ministry volunteers. The recently hired Catholic chaplain at the prison organized us volunteers into teams who would go into the prison and conduct Communion services every Saturday on two different yards. Each team of two would go in once a month. The chaplain was spread thinly among the five yards within the prison, and an active group of volunteers could make Catholic services available to more inmates. There were priests who faithfully came to the prison as often as possible to hear confessions and say Mass, but otherwise the chaplain was pretty much a one-man show for all things Catholic for over five thousand inmates.

With some apprehension, my husband and I accompanied the chaplain on our first Saturday. As we followed him around to the services we would soon be conducting on our own, I wrote everything down. Where to park. What to wear. What to bring and not bring. What gates to enter. When to show our IDs, for which we'd been fingerprinted and run through a law enforcement database. We worried that we would make a wrong turn and get lost somewhere dangerous. We thought that we'd never get used to the security measures. We suspected that we'd made a flawed decision to volunteer here. We steeled ourselves to come face-to-face with inmates.

When they arrived in the chapel, we greeted them. They seemed glad to meet us. They didn't seem much different from non-incarcerated people. In fact, they were pretty much *regular people*, except they all wore the same clothes and had done something punishable by time in prison.

The services were reverent yet vibrated with the presence of the Holy Spirit. The choir sang like angels. It was, for us, an extraordinary spiritual experience, and we knew we'd be back. God was speaking to us here, incongruously but clearly. Somehow we felt like we'd come home.

Our group of volunteers was like a family. We met monthly and determined who went in when. We read the coming Sunday readings together—although we went in on Saturday, we used the Sunday lectionary for our services—and discussed how to present the themes and lessons in the readings to incarcerated men. We helped coordinate special events, such as retreats or celebrations, two of the favorites being Our Lady of Guadalupe and Holy Thursday's Washing of the Feet. Sometimes outside groups came to give inmate retreats, and we helped by giving talks, being group leaders, donating supplies, and offering lodging to the visitors.

When I took a job in a Records office at the prison, I was able to volunteer an additional two weekdays after work. On Tuesdays, I helped facilitate a Criminals and Gangmembers Anonymous (CGA) meeting, a 12-step program that originated in prison. On Wednesdays, I led an additional Communion service in the chapel.

Detention ministry was a strange landing for someone whose previous ministries mainly involved children. The fact that I felt more at home in a prison chapel than I did in my own parish provided a trinity of proofs: that God has a sense of humor, that Jesus meant the thing about visiting him in prison literally, and that the Holy Spirit, when asked, will always provide the necessary gifts to make the impossible possible.

Working with inmate files in Records, however, did not allow me to romanticize or trivialize why these men were here. While a few may have been imprisoned unjustly, most of them were here for good reason. Some inmates continued their life of crime from captivity and had no interest in rehabilitation. Many lived the revolving-door experience, returning to prison for a new crime or parole violation within months (or weeks!) of their release.

Most inmates just wanted to do their time quietly, without attracting notice. Many of the inmates I met were just unlucky. But for circumstances, they could be you or I in our early twenties, getting caught for doing something stupid and unable to afford a decent lawyer or even to comprehend the language of law. And some inmates really did see a prison term as a giant wake-up call from God. They read voraciously, participated in every service and program offered, took (or taught) sacramental preparation classes, and opened their hearts wide to *metanoia*, to daily conversion. They lived an examined life. Some very spiritual people went by a number rather than a name. I believe I saw the face of Jesus in them far more often than they saw the holy in me.

Some diocesan offices of Detention Ministry have been renamed for Restorative Justice, because this is a more effective endeavor. While detention ministry clearly serves those held in jails and prisons, restorative justice seeks both to facilitate restitution for victims of crime and to emphasize rehabilitation over retribution for the convicted. This builds a more constructive and compassionate society.

Another group that could be touched by God's love and forgiveness through restorative justice was the correctional staff. I was sometimes aware of officers who listened with casual intensity during our services and who came to treat us volunteers with respect rather than with the initial skepticism that usually greeted our bleeding hearts. I hoped they were moved to treat the inmates in their care more humanely. I was often touched when, during the Prayer of the Faithful at our services, inmates prayed for the well-being of the officers and other staff at the prison. They also regularly prayed for the victims of their crimes. These were not prayers I would have imagined coming from the lips of criminals.

During services, we sang, repented, praised God, proclaimed the word, prayed, and shared the Eucharist together in an unlikely community of faith. Each week I prepared a reflection on the readings for the coming Wednesday. I searched for words that were relevant and helpful, while praying that the Holy Spirit would smooth my delivery. When I asked for my fellow worshippers' thoughts at the end of mine, the responses often threw sparks of wisdom and insight. *Why are you here?* I sometimes wanted to ask the speaker.

But I didn't. The things I had to know for my job did not apply to ministry. Every so often an inmate told me his commitment offense, but it wasn't information I needed. It was evidence of grace that when I went into the prison as a Catholic volunteer, I was more powerfully aware of God's love for us than anywhere else I went. I don't know why. I can't explain it. It makes no sense. I knew that when I shook hands at the sign of peace or placed Communion into upturned palms, I was touching hands that had robbed, beaten, cheated, murdered, and molested. That's when I was filled with the true mystery of sharing the Eucharist in community, because I was able to grasp those hands with love and knew that what they had done didn't matter. Where they were going, what they were going to do next, mattered. I still believe that hands that have caused hurt always have the God-given potential to be hands of tenderness.

Detention ministry gave me far more than I gave others. I felt guilty when I was thanked for doing something that so enriched my faith. Which is exactly the feeling that people devoted to various other ministries tell me they have when, for example, they go into nursing homes, places I avoid. And despite my enthusiasm, some people who have tried on detention ministry have found it an uncomfortable fit. As St. Paul writes in his first letter to the Corinthians, "There are different kinds of spiritual gifts but the same Spirit" (1 Cor 12:4).

"CAUTION: ROUGH ROAD AHEAD" read the sign I passed every morning on my way to work, just before driving through the front gate of the prison. To us employees, it meant that the state was still remiss in repaving the weather-ravaged main road. But I often wondered how the warning struck others who entered here, both arriving inmates and their visitors. I wondered if their hearts hurt at the aptness of the metaphor. Sometimes I wondered how unwitting the metaphor really was, or if someone high up in the warden's department was a bit of a poet.

There is no denying that prison is a rough road. But like the disciples on the road to Emmaus, our choice of traveling companion makes all the difference.

Christmas in Captivity

It was mid-December, the air chilled and hopeful. Advent was more than half over. We had already celebrated St. Nicholas and Our Lady of Guadalupe, so the big December event was really almost here. It was almost Christmas! My youngest daughter was at home, putting the stamps on our stacks of almost-late Christmas cards, some of which had to travel to the other coast and beyond. My older daughters would be arriving home soon, with stylish haircuts and mysterious gifts and tales of the big cities in which they now lived. Our tree was decorated; our outside lights blazed into each dark night. I had a shopping list waiting in my car for a last-minute trip to the grocery store to replenish the ingredients for the final batches of Christmas cookies: pounds of flour and brown sugar, a dozen more eggs, bags of walnuts and dried cranberries and chocolate chips, a bottle of peppermint extract. Before all that, though, I had something to do: a Communion service at the state prison, where I was a volunteer with the Catholic chaplain.

I was not allowed to bring food into the prison, or I would have brought some of the holiday treats that one customarily brings to the homes of friends at Christmas time: homemade cookies or eggnog or even candy canes. I brought in only a prayer book and my volunteer badge, a stripped-down version of the things I usually carried. All of the stuff that I brought everywhere, my wallet and phone and purse, stayed in the car. The state was very strict about what came in and just as strict about what went out. I brought in good intentions; I brought out fresh faith.

In the chapel on the medium security yard that morning, before our service started, three inmates were unpacking and setting up a Christmas tree. As they fitted the parts together, I saw that the tree was short, spindly, anemic, unloved. It had a Charlie Brown quality, even though it was artificial. The men took ornaments from a box, strung a metallic garland through the tree's branches, and affixed a star with a picture of an angel on it atop the highest point. Which would have been shorter than they were had it not been on top of a table. They worked assiduously, with a minimum of conversation, placing their decorations and then leaning back to judge the exact position-ing. They handled the shiny balls and ribbons tenderly, those hands that had somehow violated the law.

The men wore matching blue shirts and pants that said "PRISONER" in unmistakable block letters down one leg. They had very little to call their own. They occupied one of the lowest rungs of society's ladder, and perhaps deservedly so. Yet their delicate care as they trimmed the prison tree, as they moved on to arrange the figures of the shepherds and animals and new parents in the crèche, moved me to brief tears. These particular inmates were changed and humbled men. They had done wrong, but they had also worked to make some form of restitution. They were, collectively, in the hands of God: their faith stigmatized them in the eyes of other pris-oners on the yard. Within the manger scene, they placed and moved and placed again the lit-up angel, the sanitized shepherds, the animals that didn't smell, the parents who were not afraid, all awaiting a baby whose breath was destiny.

Their holy task completed, the three men slapped each other on the back. They knew that the beautifully wrapped packages under the tree were empty, were not for them. Yet they had positioned them artistically, reverently, as though to please unseen children. They honored, in this blessed place of opposites, the spirit of Christmas, the poverty of the first Christmas, with their very lives, in a way that we on the outside possibly do not. It occurred to me that maybe we cannot understand what it means to stand stripped naked before God, to have nothing left to offer but a willingness to try again. We may not comprehend exactly how forgiving God is.

As usual, after the service, the inmates thanked me profusely for coming in, and, as usual, I felt undeserving of their thanks. They had, as usual, taught me well today. Their grace in dismal circumstances made me realize that I got too caught up in the cookies and the cards; I didn't have time for silence or salvation. It was almost Christmas, and as I headed to the grocery store still feeling the pressure of those hearty handshakes on my hand, I prayed for simplicity. I prayed to be able to mind the things that matter that Christmas and to put aside the things that didn't. I prayed to remember, amid my own family festivities and Christmas cheer, the empty packages under that spindly tree and the faces of those who yearned for, and who believed in, rebirth.

A Thief in the Night

My oldest daughter was mugged one Saturday night. She was talking with a friend in the parking lot of a restaurant in Los Angeles before saying goodbye for the evening. Two young men approached her and asked her for a light, and as she offered her lighter, there was suddenly a gun at her head. Then they fled with her and her friend's purses. She said it was as quick as that: the hit-and-run death of her innocence.

My first thought, when she called in a shaky voice to tell us what had happened to her, was of gratitude to God that she had not been hurt or killed. My second thought was of vengeance. My third thought was of shame at my second thought, even though my second thought was sticking around. My fourth thought was of confusion. My fifth was a conscious decision to go back to the first thought and stay there for a while.

My husband and I had been spending time with criminals just like the two men who made our daughter a victim. We assisted in Communion services one Saturday a month at the state prison and had been surprised and humbled by the spirituality amongst the incarcerated. But after getting my daughter's phone call, I worried that the next time we volunteered, I might look at each inmate differently. So far, I had been able to separate the men from their pasts: when it came to how they got to prison, we had a "don't ask, don't tell" policy. So far, that had worked. Now I was afraid I would look at each man and wonder, Did you hold a gun to someone's daughter's head? Did you threaten to kill her? Did you steal from her not just her wallet, but her faith in the goodness of humanity?

And: was I coddling my daughter's enemy, and so being disloyal to her?

I knew that someday, should those two young men continue on the path of thievery that they had chosen, I could very well, within the confines of the prison, be giving Communion to my daughter's attackers. Which gave me pause. Which haunted my thoughts. Which complicated my relationships with the inmates and with my daughter and with God.

An honest cyclist returned my daughter's purse the next morning. It was flung by the side of the road, with car keys, checkbook, and empty wallet; without cell phone, driver's license, and her small amount of cash. My daughter said that those guys foolishly mugged the two brokest chicks in LA. She seemed to be holding up remarkably well, a real trouper, and yet she told me that the first thing she wanted to do was buy a new wallet. The recovered one was tainted with the memory of feeling powerless. She had different purses she could use, but she only had one wallet. Even touching it, she said, was creepy. Which told me that her healing was still a way off.

As was mine. The crime, of course, was hers to forgive, not mine, and yet I was wondering if I should stop going to the prison. At Mass during the week, I prayed for clear and simple answers. The gospel reading was from Luke: "If the master of the house had known the hour when the thief was coming, he would not have let his house be broken into. You also must be prepared, for at an hour you do not expect, the Son of Man will come" (Luke 12:39-40). Great, I thought, a crime metaphor. The thief in the night had taken what was not his from my daughter, had made her feel vulnerable, had made her wary of being kind, and I got to give him Communion the following Saturday. I thought about how we had been busy all week replacing what she lost, arranging for a new cell phone, a new license, a new health insurance card, all of which robbed us of more money and time. She had gone through books of mug shots at the police station, certain that she recognized one guy, only to find that her friend had identified a completely different face. The thieves, at least for the time being, remained at large in the shadows of the night, free to prey on others. Would justice ever be done?

My answer came at the end of the Gospel reading, and I almost missed it as I remained wrapped in my own angry thoughts: "Much will be required of the person entrusted with much, and still more will be demanded of the person entrusted with more" (Luke 12:48).

Once again, the wisdom of Christ blindsided me.

So much has been given to me: life, love, children, health, wealth, freedom, privilege. I return so few of my gifts to God; in fact, I hoard them. My involvement in prison ministry required an embarrassingly small amount of time and effort and presence. Any good I may have done was equally small. I believe we are called to visit the imprisoned; I believe I heard that call clearly. And it's not complicated, unless I make it that way. Jesus did not say, "When I was in prison, you made excuses for me, you condoned my crimes, you sprang me by smuggling in a fake ID." What he said was, "I was . . . in prison, and you visited me" (Matt 25:35-36).

To visit: that's all he's asking. But by treating inmates like fellow human beings, by focusing on rehabilitation and amends, by bringing Christ to the hearts and lips of those who are so often unloved and unreachable, who lack the freedom and privilege I take for granted, perhaps future crimes would be averted and future victims avoided. Perhaps minds and behaviors could be changed. Perhaps someone else's daughter would go home unaccosted, and in that way I could continue to visit the imprisoned and still look my own daughter in the eye.

The results of our visits we will never know. I only know that much has been entrusted to me, and so even more will be demanded. And that I have an awful lot of work to do before I will ever be ready for that unexpected hour.

Unforgiven

"I trust in the mercy of God forever."
—Psalm 52:10

"I think about the guy whose life I took. Because of my action, he will never be a father. I think about his wife. Did she ever find somebody else? She was young, but still. Does she sleep alone every night? Is she scared? Does she have money problems?

And I finally get what they mean when they ask me at my parole hearings if I have 'insight' into my crime. I have insight, you know what I'm saying?"
—"J," CDCR inmate

"To err is human; to forgive, divine."
—Alexander Pope

To be forgiven is a deeply ingrained human need: in the Our Father, forgiveness is mentioned just after "daily bread." Perhaps forgiveness is bread for the soul. When we pray the Our Father, we ask God to forgive us in exactly the same vein that we forgive others, which, for most of us, is a pretty risky thing to ask. I still haven't quite forgiven my brother for boycotting my sister's wedding. I haven't forgiven the two guys who robbed my daughter at gunpoint. I have barely forgiven my husband for telling me that my new haircut looked "mature." I am in big trouble if God is going to forgive me my sins the way I forgive others, which is why I prefer to pray for God's mercy and compassion.

For us flawed humans, mercy and compassion are important steps on the path to forgiveness: we must embrace the power that comes from the seemingly meek act of "turning the other cheek." We need to practice letting go. A further step is to lose our fear of empathy. When we empathize, we find more forgivable the things we can imagine ourselves doing. We've all had bad days when we've done something foolish in traffic because we weren't paying attention to our surroundings. We know what it's like to be overburdened, overstressed, overtired, overwhelmed, and so we can summon some understanding when we see these shortcomings manifested in others. But we have not all committed murder. Murderers, we agree, commit unforgivable acts: a life taken cannot be given back. We can perhaps picture ourselves in certain specific instances of life-taking: we can understand a drunk driver, whose crime arises from muddled judgment, better than a suicide bomber, whose crime arises from misguided zeal. But the murderers I know, and with whom I have become close, are the most unforgiven people I have ever met.

Not that all of the inmates who attended the Criminals and Gangmembers Anonymous (CGA) meetings for which I volunteered were murderers. Some were drug dealers or embezzlers, spouse abusers or chronic thieves, rapists or arsonists. To be honest, I didn't ask. As a volunteer with the Catholic chaplain, I was only there as a fellow believer, to share the faith journey within the structure of a 12-step program. The inmates were there, of course, as criminals and gangmembers who wanted to begin with step 1, to recognize that their lives had become unmanageable, and so there were no protestations of innocence or of having been framed. But concerning the details of their specific criminal activities, I only knew what was freely offered during the meetings: crime and shame and a prevailing acceptance that what they had done could not possibly be forgiven.

Forgiveness for their crimes, after all, was out of their hands. The people who could forgive them, their victims or the families of victims, often attended the inmates' parole hearings to make sure that the crime was neither forgotten nor forgiven. And who could blame them? To forgive the most grievous harm of the violent death of a son or a daughter, a husband or a wife, a father or a mother, seems impossibly superhuman, which is to say, divine. We humans are not capable of such forgiveness, and so we should not even be asked.

Except that's exactly what God asks of us.

Most inmates neither expect nor even dream of being forgiven by the victims of their crimes or by their own family members whom they have let down or hurt. To be forgiven by another is out of one's control, and possibly pie in the sky, which is why, in our meetings, we focused on forgiving ourselves and those wrongs that had been done to us.

And Lordy, had some of these men been harmed. From inmates I heard the most heart-stopping stories of bad and neglectful parenting, the most horrific tales of brutality by authorities that I had ever imagined. Some of these men had been so physically, emotionally, spiritually, psychologically, and sexually abused that it had long been an act of bravery just to get up in the morning. These stories, oddly enough, were usually offered not as excuses for criminal behavior, but under the broad category of Things That Suck. An absent father, a drug-addicted mother, a fist-happy cop: they just sucked, man. It was a moment of shining grace to watch a person realize that these were actually terrible injustices done to him that he had the power to forgive. That the Things That Suck could be forgiven, had to be forgiven if one was to move forward in the quest to change. And that bestowing forgiveness was liberating, invigorating, and life-altering: true grace from a steadfast God.

Forgiving themselves was much harder.

I once heard Sister Helen Prejean speak about how we rationalize our inclination to classify inmates as less-than-human, which then makes it okay to deprive them of their human dignity. Imagine, she said, the worst thing you have ever done in your life. Call to mind the thing you did whose memory makes you the most ashamed, embarrassed, or regretful. Hold it in your mind, even though you'd rather not. Now imagine that that thing is the only definition the world accepts or understands of who you are. Nothing else about you is known or matters one bit. That, she said, is often what it is like to be a convicted criminal in our society. There are no second chances for you in people's minds, no mitigating circumstances, no pity, and sometimes no true justice. You remain unforgiven.

So imagine, further, that your permanent record of the wrongs you'd done to others over the years accompanied you everywhere you went: the time you cheated on a geography test in fifth grade; the time you stole a magazine because it had a picture of a hot movie star that you wanted; the time you told everyone it was Elliott who spilled the beans about who pulled the fire alarm, not you, and labeled Elliott as a snitch forever; the time you didn't pick up the phone even though you knew it was your mother; the time you "forgot" to declare some extra income on your federal tax return—all the times you hurt feelings or broke rules or behaved badly. You know you are more than the sum of those things, that you are not the same person who did those things, that you have learned many lessons from many mistakes, but society insists on defining you by your permanent record. Even worse, imagine that the kid whose test you copied, the store owner you stole from, Elliott himself, the IRS auditor, even your own mother show up periodically to testify to your badness, to make sure that people you've met since those times know exactly what you've done and also condemn you for all of it.

Talk about Things That Suck. Just the imagining leaves me breathless.

Many convicts have been conditioned to think of themselves as chronically unforgivable by their victims, by their families, by their communities. They think of being unforgiven as sort of their natural state. Some of them are convinced that the things they have done are so wrong that not even God could forgive them. The ghosts of their victims sometimes sit next to them during our meetings, their hands folded, their breath stilled. So the men don't really see the point of forgiving themselves. It reeks of a self-indulgent, Oprah-like, empty ritual that has no application to them. They are bad. "Nothing good ever come of my life, you know what I'm saying?" a young man asked me recently. I knew it was a rhetorical question, since "you know what I'm saying?" punctuated every single one of his sentences, but I thought, "No. No, I don't know what you're saying, because in spite of your defeated expectations, there is good come of your life. Despite your self-image, there is good in you."

We cannot truly love those whom we cannot forgive, and that includes ourselves. Loving ourselves is another of those touchy-feely, silly-sounding concepts, but if we fail to love and forgive ourselves, we fail everyone else in our lives. We have to start at home, from scratch, at rock bottom: Do I love myself? Can I love myself? Am I capable of forgiving myself? Where do I begin? Am I just trippin'?

In our CGA meetings, a good place to start turned out to be the parable of the Prodigal Son. In a roomful of prodigal sons, men whose judgmental older siblings had written them off but whose mothers often still wrote letters or came to visit, the story of the boy who squandered his inheritance and ended up glad to have work in a pig sty really resonated. The boy who did everything wrong, whose behavior was shameful and scandalous, was a sort of Everyman for this audience. But the boy in the story then took the unbelievable chance of opening himself up to his father's wrath and judgment. He returned home. He figured he had little to lose. He didn't expect to be forgiven or welcomed back into the family; he merely requested a shot at a job. But his father celebrated his return with feasting and an outpouring of love. In his total vulnerability, the boy was able to accept the blanket of forgiveness in which his father wrapped him. He would still face the judgment of others, particularly in the eyes of his older brother, but his father forgave him without question, because his repentance was real, was from his heart. And in his repentance, he found the grace to forgive himself.

It can be done.

When we forgive ourselves for wrongs that we own, a small miracle happens. We learn how to pass forgiveness on to those who have wronged us. Because we have been there, we empathize with those who need our forgiveness. And we recognize that there is tremendous grace on both sides of the act of forgiveness. We are free to move to the next level of righting wrongs, which is restitution. As forgiveness becomes easier, it also seems as essential as breath, water, and bread to life. It's just that some of us have to go to prison to learn this. To *get* this.

In truth, there remained mountains to climb for CGA members who were not lifers and who would eventually be returned to their former lives. The radical changes of heart brought about in prison are not easily maintained on the outside. I thought of this recently when I was listening to a reading from the book of Ezra at daily Mass.

"My God, I am too ashamed and humiliated to raise my face to you, my God, for our wicked deeds are heaped up above our heads and our guilt reaches up to heaven. . . . But now, our God, what can we say after all this? For we have abandoned your commandments," prayed Ezra, at the end of the Babylonian captivity of the Jews (Ezra 9:6, 10). Ezra needed to say nothing after this, for the God of steadfast love had already returned the Jews to Jerusalem to rebuild the temple and to begin a new life as the holy people of God. There was one small requirement of the men of Israel, however: in order to return to the roots of their faith, they needed to leave their foreign wives and their children behind. The book of Ezra ends with a long list of the names of those men who sent away their families in obedience to a seemingly harsh God.

Many inmates can relate to this story. Often, in the quest to begin anew on the outside, they must in effect exile themselves from the world they know. The familiar neighborhoods, habits, friends, and even family members they left behind when they went to prison are sometimes major contributors to the reasons why they went to prison in the first place. The people and places they know are toxic to the new life they would like to lead. Many inmates become fearful as their release date approaches, because they doubt their own power to stick by the changes they have made while in prison. As miserable as life behind bars can be, its regimentation and restrictions can make the straight and narrow path seem like a cakewalk compared to the hazards, temptations, and self-doubt waiting on the outside. The CGA program treats crime as an addiction. The old patterns and rationalizations need to be examined, understood, and discarded. Much like a recovering alcoholic is smart to stay away from bars, a recovering criminal needs to break away from the lure of potential criminal acts. Which is sometimes the only environment criminals have ever known and the one in which they will be promptly deposited upon their release from prison. Much like the Israelites at the time of Ezra, the inmate endeavoring to begin anew must place his will in the hands of a loving, yet exacting God.

In order not to become a disheartening statistic of recidivism, he will also need his understanding of forgiveness to not desert him in times of stress or trouble. He will need to cling to his sense of himself as a forgiven person, as a beloved child of God. He will need to walk in a new direction, as well as to continue working his steps with a sponsor he trusts. He will need prayer, his own and ours, always.

"Forgive us our trespasses, as we forgive those who trespass against us," we pray, often by rote, but then we must behave in a way that makes that prayer meaningful. We must actually *forgive* those who trespass against us and ask forgiveness of those whom we have hurt, if the Our Father is to make any sense at all. We must believe, deeply and passionately, in a God who forgives. We must trust in a God who extends the possibility of redemption to everyone, no matter how long his rap sheet, no matter how unforgivable his crime, no matter how unreachable his heart. To a God who is love, not one of us is unlovable.

A Congress of World Religions

I didn't know that a prison yard was going to be a congress of world religions until I got there. In that nation of twelve hundred incarcerated souls, layered two-by-two in eight different dorms, there were reverent members of many faiths. There were Catholics, Protestants, Muslims, Mormons, Jews, Hindus, Buddhists, Druids, Odinists, Native American Spiritualists, Wiccans, Satanists, Atheists, and Toastmasters. All right, Toastmasters is not a religion, but they were the newest group on the yard. The Dungeons-and-Dragons guys were pretty fervent, too, but I didn't think they considered their pastime a religion. Yet.

The yard I worked on was like a living representation of one of those "COEXIST" bumper stickers that uses religious symbols to spell the word. You know, the *C* is a Muslim crescent moon, the *O* is a peace sign, the *X* is a star of David, and the *T* is a cross. Worship in prison required the same kind of compromise. There were several chaplain positions that often went unfilled—Jewish, Muslim, Catholic, Protestant, Native American—and the chaplains were supposed to cover the spiritual needs of all five yards in the prison. Religious volunteers came in weekly to lead some of the other groups' services. Still others were do-it-yourself, inmate-led gatherings. There were three chapels on my yard, one Catholic, one Protestant, and one small Inter-Faith, but there was talk of making all three spaces nondenominational in order to accommodate all kinds of services without offending anyone's religious sensibilities. This proposal in itself, of course, offended people.

I was familiar with this meeting of world religions because in the library, I was a pushover for the sob stories of the various chapel clerks. Since the chapel copy machine seemed to be in a permanent state of disrepair, I sometimes (always!) made copies for the different denominations. I copied the guitar chords to "Amazing Grace" and the words to Buddhist chants, the list of people fasting for Ramadan and the key to Druid symbols, sometimes all in one morning.

I got to see how people of many faiths could get along in very close quarters. I also saw the power struggles that seemed to go hand in hand with organized religion, no matter where the church was located. Some groups were more prone to infighting and massive reorganization, while some just seemed to keep on keeping on, no matter who was running the show. The yard was a microcosm of the town of which it was not really a part. I lived in a town of many churches, a church on every corner, almost more churches than residents, and I'd seen the faithful of various denominations melt down and switch allegiances and sue each other and rename their facilities. I'd also seen small communities do an awful lot of good for others. It was the same in prison.

People in trouble often turn to God, and the God of second chances is a strong figure in prison. Prisoners have a lot of time to rethink their lives and reevaluate where they've taken seriously wrong turns. There is perhaps a higher percentage of soul-searching among the incarcerated than among the outside population, and there might be a lesson there. The different faith groups on the yard were there by government mandate, but they were also there for spiritual awakenings. As was God, always and everywhere.

I believe in one God, and I figured most of these guys did, too, even though they had different names and images for the Creator. I also figured that, no matter what our creeds, if we were honest enough to recognize our faith as a humble thing, we definitely had one prayer in common: "I do believe; help my unbelief!"

Normal/Not-Normal

This is normal in prison: impossibly young men—boys, really—with wrinkly, angry, circular scars on their necks or collarbones that can only have come from bullets. Or faces and bodies so covered with tattoos that no natural color of flesh is visible.

This is normal: every single piece of office equipment or cleaning product or vocational tool or medical implement numbered and inventoried and checked several times a day. If something goes missing, a suture kit or a lawn mower blade or a flash drive, the yard is placed on lockdown and searched until it is found.

This is normal: no touching. No pats on the back, no shaking hands, no hugs, no physical contact. Of any kind. Ever. Prison is the human equivalent of those monkey studies, done in the last century, where young monkeys were never touched or cuddled or given any maternal physical contact and subsequently became maladjusted at best, intensely disturbed at worst. People need the comfort and security and intimacy of human touch. People who are never touched grow to think of themselves as unworthy of touch, as unworthy to touch. Not touching is not healthy.

This is normal: bad childhoods. Unbelievably bad childhoods. Anecdotally, I'd say most prisoners come from horrific childhood experiences, enduring the kind of parental behavior that is illegal and immoral. Tragically, the generations perpetuate the cycle of trauma. I heard stories of fathers beating their children until bones were broken and the children then having to lie about the cause of their injuries, of mothers turning tricks in front of their children in exchange for drug money, of fathers and mothers sexually abusing their own children, of emotional and physical neglect that could break your heart. Many inmates have never met their fathers. Many of them have been victims of neglectful or abusive foster placements. Many of them never got a birthday present, never learned to read, never had a home address. These stories make clear why membership in a gang would be attractive.

This is normal: addiction. Many, many crimes are the result of drugs, either the need for more drugs, or a misunderstanding involving drugs, or a drug deal gone bad, or a drug-induced haze of non-reality. Many involve alcohol: the need for more alcohol, or drunk driving resulting in a police chase or a death, or drunken fights, or alcoholic blackouts. An inmate without a substance abuse problem is not normal.

This is normal: pepper spray. It's dark orange. It smells funky. Even a hint of it makes you cough, makes your eyes water and your nose run. Then it seeps into the back of your throat and chokes you. You panic that you can't take a deep enough breath to keep you from dying. Amazingly, some prisoners have developed immunity to the stuff due to repeated exposure, which I cannot imagine. Officers carry large cans of pepper spray, although they have a fancier name for it, on their person. They use it to subdue unruly inmates or to gain control of riotous situations. Anyone who works on a yard is pretty used to moving swiftly to avoid its trail. One day in the Records office, however, an officer bumped into a desk and accidentally set off his spray. We choking clerical workers all took a long break outside while the office furniture and equipment were sanitized. Then we had a good story to tell.

This is normal: dogs that aren't playful. In prison, you assume they are working canine officers, sniffing for drugs or cell phones. You don't pet them.

This is normal: toilets in plain sight. Pooping with an audience. Most men are used to urinating in public bathrooms next to each other, but the lack of privacy around all bathroom bodily functions must take some getting used to. Among many not-normal protocols in prison, it is common courtesy to flush the toilet repeatedly during a bowel movement: with every deposit, one immediately flushes in an effort to minimize offensive odors in close quarters. The library men's room was on the other side of my office. After catching two amorous inmates in there at the same time, I restricted bathroom use to my clerks, and it became one of the perks of working in the library: a semi-private moment alone in a bathroom. The window was painted half-way up, so I didn't over-witness, but I got used to hearing "*flush—flush—flush—flush—*" every time someone was in there for more than a minute. This prison etiquette caused one mother to freak out: One of my clerks, who was back in prison for another term, told me he had trouble breaking this bathroom habit after he'd been released to the streets and was living with his mom. "WHY THE HELL ARE YOU FLUSHING SO MUCH?" she yelled at him. What's normal in prison is not normal at your mom's house. Especially when your mom has to pay the water bill.

This is normal: institutional food. Bland food on a budget. Meals in prison had to meet strict nutritional requirements, but no more. Inmates bought their own spices to give their food flavor and palatability. They could purchase additional food at the canteen or through mail-order packages, but these extras required money on their books. They also tended to be junk food and/or highly processed.

The kosher, vegetarian, or halal dietary choices were fresher and more appetizing, but permission for any such special status required a chaplain to sign off on the religious designation. I once copied an appeal for an inmate who had been denied kosher status. He thought the rabbi's refusal had been unjust. "Or it might be that swastika tattoo on your neck," I ventured.

On the main kitchen's baking days, when I walked onto the yard in the morning, the blissful scent of cinnamon rolls or bread or brownies greeted me. Alas, the inmates told me, by the time these baked goods were frozen for later use and then thawed and served, the taste and texture no longer matched the aroma's torturing promise.

This is not normal: everything that is normal on the outside. Take, for example, ice. In the United States, ice is usually not an issue. It's in our freezers, available in convenience stores, distributed in restaurants, not a remarkable commodity. On my yard, however, it was like precious jewels. Giant ice machines in the kitchen dispensed these riches. Getting some of it was an ordeal. Inmates had to wait in line at arbitrary times for a cupful of ice. My clerks were usually at work during ice distribution, so I asked for a ration of ice for my workers on summer mornings. The library was not air conditioned, and in spite of the valiant efforts of several fans, it got as hot as Hades in there by the afternoon. The library had its own bright orange Igloo cooler, clearly marked, and other work areas had no problem obtaining ice for their workers. When I asked the kitchen officers for ice, though, it was like I had asked for canapés. You want *ice*? Every *morning*? What is this, a *resort*? The answer was a big negative. I was told that my clerks were only going to sell their ice on the yard, and that I was a dupe, supplying them with contraband. Then I was told that they could wait in line like everyone else, even though they were not supposed to leave their work assignment areas during work hours.

Then I was told that the library cooler could only be filled if I had a memo signed by the sergeant and lieutenant approving my request for ice. I got the memo. Then the lieutenant was transferred, so his signature was no longer valid. Had to get an updated memo. Got that memo. Then the ice machine broke. Then I discovered that the HVAC classroom had an ice machine, so I convinced the instructor to let me fill up a bag of ice every morning. Then he retired, and the machine was shut off. On and on, the summertime quest for ice. It was just *ice*, for God's sake. And ice was just one example of a hopelessly complicated commodity, of a simple request thwarted for no good reason other than the pleasure and power of thwarting.

Prison can be like Bizarro World, where everything expected and customary is upside down and backward. Prison staff live precariously in both worlds. We spend the day under rules and procedures that we consider "normal," and then we get in our cars and check our smart phones and stop in a grocery store where eight kinds of apples and twenty kinds of cheese are just sitting there, available for purchase, and we are free to do just about anything for the rest of the evening. Sometimes we wonder, how is any of this possible? Then we sleep and get up in the morning and go back inside of our own volition and become a player in Bizarro World again. Normal/not-normal as a daily reality.

It could be challenging to talk about our work to someone who knew nothing about prison other than the sensationalized movie or TV version of lock-up. If I told an amusing story about my workplace or my coworkers, the listener would sometimes stop me. "Wait, you're talking about *prisoners*?" It could be hard to convey that the people I worked with, although incarcerated, were still human beings. They had names and personalities and idiosyncrasies, just like us. All God's children, and all that, a concept that often was met with resistance.

Sometimes in Bizarro World, the prison roles are reversed. I remember the first time an inmate confided in me that he had been a correctional officer before he was convicted, but that no one knew this, because if people knew, his life would be in danger. Another told me that he had been a probation officer before being unjustly convicted for the murder of his wife and unborn child. His case was pending with the Innocence Project. When I checked their website, he was telling the truth. He'd been wrongfully convicted, and a nonprofit organization was agitating for his release. After a while, I developed a strange and probably warped practice where I would visualize the correctional officers in state-issued blues and the inmates in the green uniforms of the officers. It was easier than you might think. There but for the grace of God go I, right? I may have been onto something, as I recently read about a program in a Kentucky prison that sponsors a "reentry-to-society simulator," wherein the prison staff and those ready to parole switch roles in order to demonstrate the very real obstacles that new parolees will face when stepping back into society.

Once, during the mandated monthly training session for my inmate clerks, I had them take a test to determine what career would best suit them, which was judged according to their answers to multiple-choice questions. Ramon, who had been incarcerated for decades, achieved an unlikely result: he was encouraged to pursue a career in Corrections. He seemed a little stunned by this outcome. "I guess I have, in a way," he said. The other clerks crowed with laughter.

A terrible part of the normal/not-normal continuum was when a staff member was found to be guilty of violating the rules, or even of committing a crime, while working in the prison. As a free staff, as opposed to correctional staff, I could have been accused of the vaguely-defined infraction of "over-familiarity" every time I was nice to an inmate. I was often told I was too nice. Once one of my clerks brought me a message from an unnamed source.

"The white inmates don't like you yukking it up with the Hispanics," said the source. "They might file a complaint."

Bring it, I thought. What they called over-familiarity, I called kindness.

No complaint was filed.

But there were far more serious cases of misconduct. Staff members smuggled in drugs or gang messages or cell phones, or they engaged in sexual acts with inmates. This last was actually considered rape, as there was legally no such thing as consensual sex between a staff member and an inmate; by design of the system, every staff member had unquestioned authority over every inmate. In this configuration of the powerful and the powerless, there could be no relationship between equals.

Still, staff members thought they could outsmart the watchful authorities and get away with committing a crime among criminals. When it was someone you knew, someone you worked with and trusted, the feeling of betrayal by your co-worker was hard to shake. You'd see them get walked off the job, and you knew it was the end of a work friendship. They wouldn't be back. The Investigative Services Unit, or ISU, was a somber place that no staff member willingly visited. You were hauled there for interrogation by unsmiling officers in black shirts. The truth would out. The lawbreakers always got busted, sometimes with the help of inmate informants. It seemed unfathomable that these rogue employees would throw away a job, a career, a good retirement, and even their freedom for the sake of money. Or love. I heard about women who had babies fathered by inmates. I knew a few women who quit or retired from their state positions in order to pursue a romance. Even as we accepted the strange world of normal/not-normal as our daily workplace, the line between green and blue, under the influence of Eros, could waver and disappear.

Staff transgressions provided just another example of the fact that no matter what color the clothes, humans can be noble or ignoble, and that people are people.

Men Are from Mars . . .

As a woman working in a men's prison, I was always aware of my gender. I was old enough to be most of the inmates' mother, but I was still female, and those were in short supply. "Aren't you uncomfortable, being looked at all the time?" asked a male colleague.

To which I replied, "I'm pretty used to it."

He may not have noticed, but the outside world is not much different. We women grow up with the understanding that as soon as we exhibit any curves, we will be looked at. We will be judged, speculated about, evaluated. We are used to men talking to our chests. We notice it even when they think they are being subtle. It's important, especially in the workplace, to insist on being treated as an equal, but there is often no getting around the looking.

Working in a prison is a little like being an elementary school teacher. You spend your day in front of a captive audience that notices *everything* about you: your earrings, a change in your hairstyle or hair color, your shoes, your lunch bag, your new glasses, if you sound like you have a cold. They freak out if you are unexpectedly absent. The substitute, if there is one, doesn't do *anything* right. When you return, you face breathless questions: Where were you? Are you all right? Are you going to leave us again? You tolerate the questions and comments, but you know where to draw the line.

Another colleague once warned me that inmates treat women in one of two ways: with zero respect or with exaggerated respect. I had overheard enough conversations to understand that many of the men on the yard thought of their wives or girlfriends or baby mamas basically as the sum of their reproductive organs or as ATMs full of cash. I had also seen the exaggerated respect: men throwing themselves against the wall when I walked through a corridor, as though they wished they could turn into Flat Stanley rather than risk getting too close to my path. But they did that with all staff members, male and female. They were trained to keep their distance.

Men who do not have much contact with women outside of sexual encounters often see women in the two-dimensional psychological context of Freud's Madonna-Whore complex. Women are saintly or slutty. They are to be revered or used. There is no middle ground, no gray area between the black and the white. We women are impossible to view as regular people.

Many inmates did not have formative relationships with their mothers, which meant that their mothers were also categorized as either Madonnas or Whores. Some had seen their long-suffering, sainted mothers grossly mistreated by a succession of male partners. Some had mothers who had abused or neglected them when they were little boys. Most had subsequently not had successful or mature relationships with the women in their lives.

So it became my mission to teach the men I worked with that women were not from Venus, that we were from the planet Earth, with our feet firmly planted on the ground, just like they were. We came in just as many shapes and colors as they did. We had just as many gifts and challenges as they did. We had brains and senses of humor and opinions, just like they did. We were just as nuanced and hard to classify as men.

I wanted to show them that all women and men were aligned along the gender spectrum, sometimes in surprising ways. Just as not all men cared about monster trucks, not all women cared about nail polish colors. It astonished some of them, for example, when I could talk pro football knowledgeably or when I wasn't afraid of lizards. But I was also squeamish about violence in movies. The gender stereotypes were fluid.

Since my husband was a volunteer at the prison, we were able to model a marriage of two people who liked and loved and respected each other (most days!). Many inmates had never seen a marriage of equal partners. It was important to me that they saw us as but one example of a solid relationship, that they knew there were many such relationships in the world, and that they each deserved to be a life-giving part of such a one.

The law library gave out divorce packets every day, as many marriages that began on the outside did not survive the stress and physical separation of a prison sentence. Inmates served papers on their spouses by mail or got served through the mail by their wives. Most did not have much property or money to fight over. The more complicated filings involved children, and many inmates gave up fighting for any sort of child custody. There was nothing sadder than a defeated father who had signed away his parental rights to another, seemingly better, non-incarcerated dad.

Twice a year, it was possible for inmates to marry someone from the outside. These rare and joyful days required mountains of paperwork, but the bride was permitted to wear a wedding gown and bring in family members, and the groom was allowed to select two guests from among his peers to attend the wedding. Sometimes the lucky man was marrying a woman he'd known for a long time, and sometimes he was marrying a pen pal with whom he'd corresponded while he was incarcerated. A designated staff member was deputized to perform weddings on behalf of the county.

Because my yard was SNY, there was the occasional transgender inmate who was transitioning from male to female. These inmates were housed in men's prisons until they were surgically certified as women, but often they were in the process of taking hormones and presenting themselves as female. The library offered resources to them, reading material and helpful addresses to which they could write for support. Sometimes they just wanted some girl talk. The library became known as a place where all were welcome, where information was valued and available, and where slurs against any ethnicity or religion or gender or nationality or sexual orientation would get you kicked out.

The line between inclusive and permissive was a fine one, and I walked it carefully. I tried to be helpful and fair both to the inmates and the correctional officers, and both groups usually treated me with the respect I showed them. On good days, I kept my balance. On bad days, I tried to remember that whatever lousy thing was going on and driving me crazy would eventually be resolved. As an unapologetic liberated woman, I held all the men I worked with to a high standard, which they met, even if they secretly thought I was the biggest b-word they'd ever known.

. . . *Women Are from Venus*

On the other hand, as one of the few women on the yard in daily contact with inmates, I was not against the practice of manners. Or perhaps by manners, I mean gallantry. I thought it appropriate to thank a man for holding the door for me or to allow one of my clerks to carry a heavy box of books across the room for me, even though my arm muscles were perfectly capable of lugging it myself. I thought that these gender-encoded manners could lead to an awareness of, as well as a solicitude for, the well-being of other people, even if they seemed dated. I thought that a demonstration of old-fashioned manners—the small, please-and-thank-you, polite treatment of others—might soften the edges of some of these seemingly hardened men. My silent mantra: kindness begets kindness.

My favorite act of gallantry was a downright quaint custom that began with Karma, who was a gardening genius. Since our yard was designated as medium security, some plants and small trees and grass were permitted to grow, as opposed to the unrelieved concrete expanses of the maximum security yards. Karma had managed to enlist a crew to break up the drought-stricken hard earth and had planted rows of flowers outside the library (do not ask where the seeds came from). He'd casually dug up rose bushes from other areas of the yard and transplanted them to flank the library door. This patch of color and beauty delighted me as I walked into work each morning. Upon discovering a plastic vase in my office one day (do not ask where it came from), I cut a few budding roses for my desk.

When Karma noticed what I'd done—because any different thing I ever did was noticed—a tradition was born. After that, as long as there were flowers blooming outside, there was an arrangement in my office. When Karma paroled, he made sure to include the required flower arranging in the new clerk's unwritten job duties.

Not many women can say, as I can, that for a golden period of time, men gave me flowers every day. Fortunately, I have a very understanding husband.

Institutionalization

Lifers dread the use of the word "institutionalization" at parole hearings, as it is a code word indicating a denial is coming. It means that an inmate has lived so long within the confines of the prison system that he will not be able to function properly or lawfully in free society, that he requires the continued constraints of the institution. A day in prison is so rigidly controlled and structured and dictated that a prisoner loses the ability to make decisions for himself. A prisoner does what he is told, if he knows what's good for him, which is not conducive to the development of strong critical thinking skills.

Institutionalization made sense to me, because working in that environment forty hours a week made me realize that, every now and then, I was beginning to think like an inmate. One day we received a box of newspapers that were tied together with string. STRING! At home I have a large ball of white string in the kitchen drawer. I rarely use it ever since the post office outlawed it on packages. I think it came in handy once all last year, to tie the two halves of an antique molded cake pan together, as directed by *The Joy of Cooking*, while the cake baked. Here in prison, however, actual string is precious. Technically it is contraband, which is why the inmates figured out how to make string out of plastic trash bags. I never understood the process by which they accomplished this invention, but the end result functioned like actual string. We used to it hang bulky mandatory legal notices on the bulletin board, and for various repairs.

But this was honest-to-God string that had come in the mail. I was oddly excited to see it, and to slip it from the newspapers. I did this quickly and smoothly, moving it furtively from the box and stashing it in the back of my middle drawer, where it made a little string-nest among the stamp pads. I sensed the inmate code of behavior at work in my actions: *No extraneous movement. Don't draw attention to yourself.*

This was how I knew periodically that I needed a vacation.

Eat a Peach

The thing I remember best about Louie is that he said he hadn't had a peach in thirty years. Louie was a lifer; in his fifties, he had been in prison since his twenties. On the day he told me this, as he was hanging out in the library, a couple of landscape workers were ripping out two trees in the chapel courtyard. The trees had grown from saplings and had now turned out to be fruit trees, suspected peach trees, and so had to be removed from the prison grounds before they bore any fruit. This is because fruit can be fermented into alcohol by inventive inmates. Which explains why Louie had not had a peach in thirty years.

Louie had recently been found suitable for parole at his Parole Board hearing, a ritual that inmates with life sentences endure every so many years. Up until the past few years, only a minute percentage of lifers in California were ever found suitable for release from prison. A typical board hearing used to end in certain denial, but the sea change in public attitude from a preference for punishment to an interest in rehabilitation, along with a federal court order to reduce the state prison population, meant that now men were sometimes emerging from their hearings with a dazed look and a piece of paper that read "Parole Granted." A waiting period of 120 days followed the board's decision, to allow for review. For a murder conviction—not all life sentences are for murder—an additional 30 days were tacked on, during which time the governor could reverse the board's outcome. Past governors had almost always taken this route; it was frankly expected. Now, however, the governor was mostly upholding the board's suitability findings, trusting the board members to do their job.

The new normal of the Parole Board prompted many lifers to take their hearings seriously for the first time in decades. They came to the library to organize their paperwork, make copies of favorable work reports and letters of support, write letters of remorse to their victims and/or their victims' families, look up addresses of helpful entities on the outside, formulate practical parole plans, and network with lifers who had already been found suitable and were somehow living through the waiting period, wanting only to stay out of trouble for their last blessedly finite days of captivity. The library had become a little hub of hope for inmates who'd never expected to feel such an emotion. They suddenly had work to do.

So Louie was spending a lot of hours in the library, killing time, talking about the past and the future, and helping some of his fellow lifers whose board dates were approaching. He talked about his family, his daughter who was now an adult, the grandkids he had yet to meet, the house his dad had left him, the work he hoped to do with at-risk young gangbangers. He had been a gangmember in his day, deviant and up to no good, until he'd been convicted of murder along with his partner in crime, or "crimee." It was hard for me to imagine Louie as a young, ruthless, and conscienceless hoodlum, because I knew him as a thoughtful, intelligent, good-humored presence on the yard. He'd obviously put his years in prison to good use. He'd gotten educated and enlightened and rehabilitated. His crimee had been released from another prison the year before. Now it was his turn.

Louie's thoughts were full of family, freedom, and peaches. He talked about looking forward to having a burger at Carl's Jr., whose relentless commercials on TV featured juicy, voluptuous meat. I reminded him that he might be better satisfied at In-N-Out, the iconic burger place of California. He'd forgotten about In-N-Out. So many possibilities! He was almost dizzy with the anticipation of such good fortune as to be able to walk into a fast-food restaurant and order *whatever the heck you wanted*. Such freedom was unimaginable after thirty years. "That's the first place I'm gonna go, the first thing I'm gonna do," he said. "In-N-Out. Where's the closest one?"

As his release date drew closer and the governor did not reverse the board's decision, as he was called in to sign his final parole paperwork and find out the day of his physical release, Louie became philosophical. "I'm looking forward to the burgers," he said on one of the last days he came into the library, "but really, the first thing I'm probably gonna do when I go through that last gate is fall on my knees and cry like a baby."

Louie's been gone for about three months now. The last time I went to In-N-Out, I pictured Louie in his parole clothes, which were probably any color but blue, with his cry-like-a-baby tears dried on the car ride, walking through the In-N-Out door, grinning when a teenager with a chipper voice asked to take his order, pulling his gate money out of his pocket and paying with money for the first time in thirty years. The thought made me appreciate a well-fried french fry like never before. I picture Louie's grandkids teaching him how to use a smart phone or how to Google. I picture him with peach juice on his chin, with a big bowl of peaches and plums and grapes and berries on the table in his home. Some people might say that Louie doesn't deserve to be out of prison, that the life he took should be paid for with his own. No one knows better than a murderer that he can never give back or fully atone for the life taken. There is nothing a murderer can do or say to bring back the dead or to erase a family's grief. But if we believe in God's redemptive love, we have to believe that every person, every single one of us, can change, can be forgiven, can be redeemed. The power of God's compassion is so much greater than ours, after all. Louie may very well alter the course of some young man's life by sharing his story, by offering his guidance, by giving the benefit of his journey of remorse and renewal. His presence may save some other precious and holy life. I may never know. I may quite probably never see Louie again. But I think of Louie every time I eat a peach, and the world seems a more hopeful place with him out there somewhere.

Family Visits

I t is well known that an inmate who maintains contact and relationships with family members has a better shot at success upon release from prison. The problem is the obstacle-laden path that families must follow to visit a loved one in prison. Prisons in California are usually situated far outside of population centers, in small towns that welcome the jobs created by a correctional institution and that are often inaccessible by public transportation. Families of limited means may not have a vehicle that can make a long drive to the boondocks or money for the gas for such a trip, let alone the price of even a cheap motel room. They may lack the ability to take time off from work to take a trip to prison. Any or all of these burdens can keep families from visiting their incarcerated loved one. Of course, they may also just be too angry with him to want to stay in touch.

Friends' and family members' applications to come inside must be screened and approved before they are permitted to visit a prisoner. Prior convictions render a visitor ineligible. Any response deemed less than true on the application is an automatic rejection. Strict rules govern what one can wear, what one can bring in, including how much money and in what denomination (to be spent on overpriced and unhealthy snack food in prison vending machines). Proper ID and the birth certificates of any accompanying minor children must be presented. Anyone other than a child's parent must have permission from a court to bring the child to visit an incarcerated parent. Any deviation of any kind from the rules means that you will not be allowed to visit, no matter how far you have come. Worst of all, there is no guarantee that family members will be treated with any degree of respect. It just depends who is working at Visiting that day.

Nonprofit programs like Get on the Bus in California bring children long distances to visit their moms and dads, but many inmates never see any members of their family. Some inmates actually prefer it that way, as they do not want their loved ones, especially their children, to see them in a prison setting. They find it humiliating. But most of the inmates I worked with looked forward to any visits, as a way to stay connected, to enjoy the food and conversation, and to relieve the loneliness and monotony of prison time. Some had visits once a year, while some, especially those from wealthier families, expected visits every weekend.

Weekend and holiday visits during visiting hours were strictly regulated and observed. Physical contact was limited to a brief hug and kiss upon arrival and departure. Handholding was permitted. Inmates were not allowed to touch money or approach the vending machines. Inmates and their visitors were not supposed to mingle or interact with other inmates and their visitors. A visit could be terminated for untold reasons. Any infractions of the prison rules could result in the suspension of visiting privileges.

Family visits were different, the holy grail of visits. On family visits, the inmate actually left the yard and spent the weekend in a special visiting facility. Only immediate family—parents, spouses, children, siblings—could visit under these circumstances, meaning that you could sleep with your wife, but not your girlfriend or your baby mama. The visitors could order food from a preapproved mail-order catalog, and the whole deal was structured to feel like spending a normal weekend at a motel. The facilities were limited, and the waiting list was long.

When I started in the library, lifers were not eligible for family visits. In light of the new philosophy resulting in the parole board finding more and more lifers suitable for parole, however, that limitation was lifted so that potential parolees could benefit from the experience of a family visit. (Inmates with convictions for sex offenses or any kind of domestic abuse were still excluded from eligibility.)

Not unexpectedly, as soon as lifers were theoretically eligible for family visits, the library had a run on marriage packets.

The department dragged its feet on implementing these new guidelines for family visits, but inmates were nothing if not adept at patience.

Just before and just after a family visit, an inmate was noticeably squirrely. He was awash in nervous anticipation before the visit and enveloped in a palpable depression afterwards. The sweetness of that little slice of normalcy made it difficult to go back to the yard. But he returned to his pals there like a conquering hero. They wanted all the details.

I had a lot of respect for those who still wanted to be a good husband or son or dad or brother while they were incarcerated. Anyone with a family knows that family relationships are fraught enough on the outside. Maintaining a family during a prison term was a noble if seemingly impossible pursuit.

A Moment of Silence

Moments of silence are usually not my favorite moments. They seem to be a second choice, a watered-down option when a prayer would be either illegal or politically incorrect. The person leading the meeting or the ceremony or whatever the occasion asks for a moment of silence, and I confess that all I hear in the silence are the unspoken questions in the speaker's mind: "How long is a moment supposed to be? Is this long enough? What shall I say to end it?" I hear the presider's brain, counting and considering, "One-Mississippi, two-Mississippi, three-Mississippi, four-Mississippi . . . OK, that's probably long enough. Is it? Hmmm. Or maybe now." When the moment of silence is finally broken, all I feel is relief.

After one night, however, I felt a bit differently. One night's moment of silence was unlike any other I'd experienced. I was at the weekly Tuesday night meeting of Criminals and Gang-members Anonymous. As a staff facilitator rather than a participant in the group, I sat in the back and did the paperwork so the CGA group could meet. Most of the group members were serving life sentences, mostly with the distant possibility of parole, although a few were LWOPs. That week being National Crime Victims Week, I had received some literature regarding commemorations and tributes around the state. Since the CGA motto is "One less crime, one less victim," I thought it would be appropriate to ask one of the group leaders to mention the week's designation and to ask for a moment of silence for all of the victims represented by the perpetrators in the room.

He obliged, making the announcement, reading from the paper I'd brought, and the room went quiet. Heads bowed. Thoughts turned inward. The moment was fully embraced. Suddenly the air was weighted with a collective heaviness of heart, in what turned out to be this extraordinary moment of silence. Part of the rehabilitative process is learning to develop empathy for what you, as a criminal, have put your victims through by your actions. This means you must take responsibility for not only your immediate victims, but also for their family, your family, and the greater society whose laws you have broken. You must be able to walk in all of those individual shoes, the ones belonging to the people to whom you have caused grave injury or death or disability or fear or material loss or psychological harm, before you can ask for forgiveness from those whom you have victimized. You must learn the meaning of compassion before you can ask for compassion. Above all, you must never forget or try to minimize the impact and consequences to others of the wrongs you have done.

I could thus imagine the many faces conjured in the minds of the sixty or so inmates present at the CGA meeting: faces of loved ones or random strangers, faces of terror or shock, faces that may haunt their dreams or inhabit their thoughts. The pain of the victims of murder, kidnapping, rape, molestation, robbery, cheating, beating, and mayhem of every kind was palpable as these men remembered the debts they will never really be able to repay. Those who suffered because of the people in that room were young, old, male, female, beloved, unknown, innocent, guilty, in the wrong place at the wrong time—all their lives taken or forever changed by the felons who bowed their heads together. The moment was collective, but each man remembered separately.

I could feel the regret rising to the ceiling of the chapel where we met. I could sense the past reaching with long fingers to tap each man on the shoulder: Remember me? Remember what you did?

Victims and their families sometimes feel they are ignored or forgotten in the rehabilitative process. They often don't want to read letters of apology from monsters; they don't want to hear about the criminal's rehabilitation; they don't want the offender ever to get a parole date; they don't want to forgive, possibly, in the case of families of murder victims, because they feel that forgiveness would be like forgetting their loved one, or worse, dishonoring him or her. But on this night, during this powerful, and surely prayerful, moment, the victims were present. This is small consolation to those who have been victimized, I know. But it is perhaps a place for healing to begin.

Along with the regret, I could also sense, rising like incense, the promise to be a better man. Call me naïve, but I believe that each man's slog through the CGA program is in response to a holy call, to be the person God created him to be, to fix whatever is broken within him, to reach for redemption. People can do truly terrible things to each other, but every soul is sacred. Every human is a beloved child of God, even the ones most of us have given up on ever reaching.

Later, back at home, I took my own moment in the silent night to pray for this earth full of grief, for victims and perpetrators, for all of our sorry souls. Then, remembering God's abiding love, which gathers all our sorry souls like a mother to her heart, I gave thanks for that night's moment of silence.

Inmate Turner

Inmate Turner (as always, not his real name) sat at a table across from another inmate. From my office window, it looked like Inmate Turner was conducting an interview. He sat with both index fingers touching his chin, listening, then asking, then a small smile. He might have been discussing his fee.

I had seen him do this before. Along with charm and loquaciousness, Inmate Turner had legal smarts. I could picture him tidied up in a business suit and tie, enticing the gullible to pull out their checkbooks. Other inmates with legal problems—and really, was there any other kind of inmate, because look where they were—basically hired him as their jailhouse lawyer. Inmate Turner was our resident legal eagle. I imagine every prison library has one. He was paid with sheets of blank paper or soups or Lord knows what else—the client's oldest male child, perhaps.

This particular inmate supplicant, or potential paying customer, had a battered accordion folder stuffed with copies and originals of his life's resume: old court minute orders, abstracts of judgment, hearing transcripts, failed writs of habeas corpus, letters from court clerks, arrest reports, trust account statements, copies of appeals, on and on. He spread some of the documents for inspection on the table in front of Inmate Turner, who glanced at one or two of them before returning to his Don-Corleone-like posture.

Would the godfather grant the proposed favor? Would he take the case? Probably, as Inmate Turner's fine hand could be seen in many of the copies of legal work that I made every day on this yard. I had first met Inmate Turner when I was also covering the minimum-security yard, but Inmate Turner had gotten himself into some kind of trouble over there and was sent to the hole. (The hole—or Ad-Seg, short for Administrative Segregation—is the place where inmate rule-breakers go while they are being investigated.) Inmate Turner said he was set up; the whole thing was a scam. But whatever he'd done got him enough points to be reclassified from minimum to medium security. Hence his presence in my library.

Inmate Turner was indefatigable in his pursuit of justice, on his own behalf and on behalf of his clients. He had several civil lawsuits pending personally, mostly suing various prison staff around the state for their alleged misconduct regarding him. His recent work on behalf of another inmate had him taking on the state of Washington, and it required my assistance in securing the proper state forms. I didn't know when he found time to work in the kitchen, which was his properly assigned prison job, because he was in the library all day long, first in, last out, five days a week. He burned through much of our allotted monthly supply of typewriter ribbons. He filled out at least one information request slip a day. He actually applied to be a library clerk, but I knew better. The library was not about to become part of "*la famiglia*."

Inmate Turner was a con man, which was exactly why he was in prison, having written some checks that were not his to write, among other crimes. "I'm a good writer," he told me. "But some of my best writing got me here." I suspected that rehabilitation held no interest for him. The thrill of the scam would always be more gratifying than the boring honest wage. This turned out to be true when Inmate Turner finally paroled, leaving several inmates behind with unfiled legal documents and much unfinished business. One inmate, unfortunately, had even had his family pay Inmate Turner with real money through some complicated mechanism of wiring money into a black hole from which it could never be retrieved. After Inmate Turner left amid promises to continue representing him on the outside, the inmate learned that he had missed all court deadlines for his appeal. He was out of luck.

Inmate Turner was a con man, but apparently not a good enough one not to get caught. His own appraisal of his talents was inflated. Not unforeseeably, Inmate Turner was back in the system within the year.

Lessons in Appreciation

I had the chance to introduce one of my clerks, Neil, to my husband, who was volunteering at the prison for an evening program. I performed the standard introduction: "Neil, this is my husband, Randy. Randy, this is my smartest legal clerk, Neil." They shook hands, exchanged pleasantries.

The next morning, Neil thanked me profusely for the introduction.

"I haven't been introduced to anyone like that for a long time," Neil said. "It was nice." His old eyes were a little shiny.

I thought he was going to say how nice it was to meet my husband, but it was the simple, formulaic, polite manners that had moved him. I often forgot that when you were a lifer with decades of incarceration under your belt, you aren't at all accustomed to common courtesy, to things we on the outside take for granted. You are used to being referred to by a number or by last name. You are used to being shouted at and belittled. You are used to treading carefully around everyone, other inmates and staff, lest you bring some unwanted trouble on your head. You are used to being invisible.

It was a big part of my mission to recognize the humanity, as well as the divine spark, in each person with whom I came in contact at my job. Certainly some of the men I met were annoying or creepy or unlikeable, but not a single one of them was unworthy of kindness. My goal was for the library to be a kind of neutral zone on the yard, a Switzerland of impartial information, a Zen retreat center of nonjudgment. My clerks knew that we were there primarily to serve the population of the yard to the best of our ability, by providing the facts, by dispelling rumors, by offering educational opportunities. But it was also important to listen respectfully to people who needed to talk and to be kind.

I wanted the library to be as unlike the rest of the prison as was possible in a place dedicated to secure incarceration. Almost like a classroom teacher, I put up seasonal decorations in the windows of my office: a string of tree lights for Christmas, bulletin board pumpkins for Halloween, tiny flags for the Fourth of July, a paper shamrock for St. Patrick, a shiny red heart for St. Valentine. They were cheap flimsy things from the Dollar Tree store, but the inmates treated them with reverence. The holidays are hard for incarcerated people, either because of all they missed out on as a child or because of what they are currently missing with their families. But I often saw that the traditional reminders of magic enchanted the little kid buried in the soul.

In return for any small gestures on my part, the gratitude I was shown often floored me. There was thankfulness for the merest trifle, for the things I usually forgot to be grateful for in my daily life. It seemed every day offered a new way for me to learn a lesson in appreciation. These guys already had it down.

The Work Glossary

tarting a new job often feels like a disaster.

Unless you have worked at the same job your entire life and qualify for the gold retirement watch, you know the unease and insecurity of starting a new position. Even if you've worked in the same career field, you may have moved to new challenges or to a different company. When you start a new job, you can count on some universal experiences. You have not slept well the night before and woke up before the alarm went off. You are either very early, having allowed too much time to commute or park, or are almost late, having not allowed enough time. You are overdressed or underdressed: what were you thinking with this outfit? You meet a dozen or so new coworkers in about two minutes and can't remember a single name. You are on your best behavior, but it seems inadequate. As you begin your training, you try to be smooth and alert and ask intelligent questions, but inside you feel overwhelmed by your apparent stupidity. You want to say, as you make your twentieth mistake, "But in my real life, I am a capable, smart person! Honest!" But you know that no one would believe you when you are such an obvious dolt. You are quite certain you have made a terrible mistake and will never, ever feel comfortable in this job.

The unfamiliar glossary of work terms can magnify that creeping feeling of apprehension when you start a new job. You know from experience that the day will come when you understand the workplace lingo and even feel comfortable using it, when you will be the one to help out a nervous new employee, who in turn will think that you really have your act together. Until that day comes, however, you are awash in the strange and unintelligible verbal shorthand of your job. You cannot follow the nonsensical conversation of your coworkers until you learn the language.

Prison is no different. Libraries are no different. Of course, making a mistake in the language of prison can seem far more consequential than messing up the language of the library. When I first worked in Records, my trainers admonished me that a mistake in paperwork could lead to the inadvertent release of a violent inmate, whose subsequent crimes would be on my head. That was sobering. There were enough acronyms and abbreviations and numerical codes and formulas to crowd other information out of my brain, but the dread of causing something terrible to happen remained.

Everything had a number, and there was a number for everything. Inmates had numbers; cases had numbers; crimes had numbers; sentences had numbers; forms had numbers. The penal code was a book full of numbers with important decimals. The Department Operations Manual used even more decimal spaces. Then there were the alphabetical mysteries. Anything that could be shortened to a few letters was forever after known only by those letters. I was given lists to familiarize myself with. I made my own lists. A supervisor's instruction might consist only of numbers and letters and connector words like "of" or "for." I felt a little bit bonkers for a while. Eventually, I could speak Prison Records like a pro.

Moving to the library position meant a whole new glossary of terms, but these seemed more familiar and more user-friendly. This might have been because libraries were second in my personal reverence of places only to churches. Although I did not have that intense desire to catalog things that seemed to motivate many of the librarians I met in the course of working in the library, I felt at home among books. And among readers.

Adding to the work glossaries that came to be at my fingertips was the glossary of inmate terms. I never became as fluent as a native speaker, but it helped my job to go more smoothly if I kept track of some of the shorthand used by the men with whom I worked. They too could speak the numbers-and-letters jargon of the official prison glossary, but they also knew how to speak in their own code. There were times I knew I didn't understand the conversation I was hearing, and I knew better than to intrude when not invited.

The inmates had a penchant for blunt nicknames, such as Baldy or Gordo (Spanish for fat). The guy they affectionately called Lefty had been born with only a right arm. I was horrified, but he was fine with it. The stranger nicknames reminded me of my dad's Navy pal Bonly Jonly, so named when he said, upon intake into the military, that his name was B.J., only B.J., the initials didn't stand for anything, and the officer wrote B(only) J(only) on his paperwork. Some nicknames are for the ages.

Spanish Lessons

As a French major in college, I knew I had an ear for languages. I picked up enough Italian after a semester in Rome to make myself understood. Learning Spanish seemed comparatively easy after French, because the Spanish language is so blessedly regular and phonetic. The rules of Spanish spelling and grammar admit to very few exceptions, which make it a joy to try to speak. I had used my rudimentary skills to communicate with Spanish speakers when I worked for the church, and my elementary Spanish came in handy in prison.

In California prisons, Latino inmates make up about 40 percent of prisoners. Many of these men who came to the US illegally and got in trouble with the law are promptly deported upon their release. Some of the Latino inmates on my yard had been incarcerated, deported, and had snuck back over the border multiple times, only to be caught up in the correctional system again. They ranged from the very young to the very old. And they spoke Spanish primarily.

Their situation made me wonder how I would fare in a second language in other circumstances like school or work or prison. Some of these guys were trying to get their GED in a second language. They fought their cases in a second language. They complied with the exacting rules and regulations of prison in a second language. They dealt with threats in a second language. It was impressive. And as fluent in English as they might become, they often preferred to speak their native language. This was also true for the inmates who spoke Tagalog or Vietnamese or Russian or any other language.

One inmate who became a daily fixture in the library spoke only Japanese. Mr. Ito was elegant and mysterious. I couldn't imagine what he'd done to get himself a sentence in a state prison, but there he was. Neil, the legal expert, figured out that he was trying to get approval to serve out his time in his own country. Mr. Ito fascinated us because he signed his trust account withdrawal slips with three beautiful, delicate, intricate characters, which for all we knew actually translated to "F*ck off." He thanked us for every service we provided with a sweet smile and a bow. I noticed that Neil bowed ceremoniously in response and realized that I did, too; you almost can't *not* bow when someone bows to you.

On the occasions that I used my halting Spanish, the responding inmates would grin broadly and release a rapid-fire stream of Spanish that I had trouble following. They figured that if I could passably ask them how many copies of a legal document they needed, I must be fluent. And of course, I wasn't. They also tried the technique of speaking their language more loudly to an uncomprehending face (mine), which also never works. Volume was not my problem; speedy mental access to vocabulary was. One of my clerks decided that the best way to help me improve my Spanish was to speak to me exclusively in Spanish. I made good progress until he was transferred.

The library sometimes sounded like a living example of either the Tower of Babel, when no one could understand each other, or Pentecost, when suddenly everyone could speak each other's language. Perhaps it was a matter of perspective: Pentecost was a good day; Babel was not.

Stumped by the Code of Prison

I am the first to admit that I failed to break the code of prison talk. I rarely understood enough of what was actually being said, and I was never fluent.

Our library code was pretty innocent. During Karma's stint as the doorman, checking inmates into the library, taking their IDs, and directing them to sign legibly on the sign-in sheet, he was adept at alerting me that someone unusual—an officer or a "suit"—was approaching the library entrance. "CA-CAW!" he'd say, not to be mistaken for an observant crow. With my library coworkers, he'd wait until they were sure to hear him, or even until after they were through the door before he'd cup his hand and call, "CA-CAW! CA-CAW!"

My own attempts to speak the language of prison fell flat. I once called a particularly trying patron a "jackrabbit," and my clerks looked confused. Then Karma burst into laughter. "It's jack*wagon*, Ms. Schultz!" he said, a word I'd heard him use all the time. I still don't know exactly what it means or its etymology. But it taught me not to appropriate a language I didn't understand. As an old white lady, it's better that I don't start rapping or introduce my husband as my baby daddy. You know what I'm sayin'?

My clerks got used to my stock response whenever they came to me with in-house squabbles or petty grievances. "Deal with it," I'd say. This phrase had worked well in parenting teenagers. After a while, each time a clerk told me some long tale of woe concerning a coworker, I'd listen respectfully. At the end of his complaint, he'd look at my face and sigh, "I know: *Deal with it.*" He usually did.

Anyone who works with young people is familiar with the extravagant use of the f-word. (When my children were very young, they thought that "fart" was the f-word, an anecdote that my clerks found hilarious.) In prison, the f-word can replace just about any part of speech: verb, noun, adjective, adverb, interjection, salutation, indefinite article. OK, maybe not that last one, but you catch my drift. I couldn't decide if it was creativity at its finest or laziness at its worst, the inventing or the stifling of a vibrant vocabulary. Maybe it was both. Overuse of the f-word was not limited to the prison population: custody staff and free staff also peppered everyday discourse with f-bombs. Once, just outside the library door, an officer went ballistic on an inmate who was not where he was supposed to be at that moment. I went to the door to see what the commotion was. The red-faced officer was berating an inmate who was known to be mentally slow. His bruising torrent of ingeniously bad language flooded over this cowering inmate, and I realized where I knew this officer from: church. He was a fellow parishioner. That seemed ironic.

My clerks were very strict with any inmates who used bad language around their boss, as though they believed that my innocent ears had never heard such language. It was another instance of them treating me like a damsel-in-distress, so every now and then, I just had to check that inclination. I'd hear them chide someone for saying something a little blue in my presence. A *lady* was present.

"Sorry, ma'am," the offender would mutter.

"Well, next time watch your f*cking mouth," I'd say, uttering the whole word for shock value.

The inmates didn't like it, but I thought of it as another good reminder that women were people, not mere helpless dolls or princesses on pedestals. A little earthiness was useful in countering their tendency to deify women.

I had to resist my own urge to act on the outside like I was some kind of badass, that I hung out with gangbangers, that I was totally hip to the lingo and experience of prison, that I was *woke*. Because I wasn't. I saw only what was shown to me. I know that my clerks often protected me from the grittiest details of their lives. I didn't really know what it was like to be incarcerated, to be a number, to be kept constantly in check, to be at the mercy of an ailing system, because I got to leave every day.

I sometimes noted that I spoke Spanish like a three-year-old, but I'm pretty sure I spoke prison-talk at that primary level, too.

The Language of Grief

When I started working at the prison in Records, I was still a religious volunteer. I was able to arrange my work hours so that I could continue to conduct the Wednesday afternoon Communion service in the Facility D chapel. My volunteering would meet a dramatic end, but that is a story for another time. This is a reflection on a different topic, which is learning to speak the language of grief.

There is so much grief and sorrow behind prison walls. Prisoners mourn the lives and families and relationships of which they've deprived themselves, although there is sometimes the faint hope that all could be restored someday. The deeper, inconsolable grief is for the loved ones who die while an inmate is incarcerated. An inmate is only rarely permitted to attend the funeral of a parent or a spouse or a child, because of the security concerns and the expense involved in such a furlough. During my time in the library, I'd never seen an inmate's request to go to a funeral granted. Most often, an inmate was summoned to the chaplain's office. The chaplain broke the news of a death in the family. The inmate was permitted to call home only after the chaplain had verified the death with the funeral home, because in the past, fake reports of deaths had been used to gain free phone calls under false pretenses. Which seemed like bad karma, but desperate people resort to desperate, unethical measures.

The bereaved inmate was then offered counseling, but often he refused the offer and withdrew from the chaplain's office. He might look for someplace quiet to process the sad news, but such a place of retreat on the yard was a rarity. He might confide in a trusted friend. He might keep it all inside and act out for a reason not apparent to anyone else. He might try to harm himself. He might go to church.

The chapel was where I often heard news of the death of a loved one, especially during the Prayers of the Faithful, when inmates voiced their poignant personal petitions and asked for the prayers of the congregation.

Throughout one spring and just into summer, I had often requested prayers for the sick and in particular for my father's failing health. The regular attendees knew that I was preoccupied with family matters, with the prospect of losing my dad. He was on dialysis, and his heart was inexorably giving out on him. On one Wednesday, as I silently prayed about my father's imminent death, my raw nerves were drawn to a song during the service:

"We hold a treasure, not made of gold,
    in earthen vessels, wealth untold . . ."*

The men in the inmate choir sang so sweetly and gently, their harmony traveling around the chapel and landing in my heart. I thought about my dad's earthen vessel, so frail, so fragile. We family members fixated on his earthen vessel; we pre-mourned the day soon to come. As strongly as I believed that my dad's soul would eternally be, I dreaded the loss of this beloved earthen vessel. I was not ready to be fatherless.

---

* John Foley, "Earthen Vessels" (Portland, OR: OCP, 1975).

To my embarrassment, the hymn got to me. I started to cry. How unprofessional, I thought, upset with myself on top of my wretchedness. Here I was supposed to be leading a Communion service, and I wasn't able to speak. Everything stopped for a few minutes as I regained some measure of composure. Gradually, miraculously, I felt encircled by brotherly compassion, cradled by the unspoken emotion of everyone who had ever lost a treasured earthen vessel. I learned that day the power of sorrow to bond us in our common humanity. The language of grief is not composed of words, but of love. This silent language can lift our spirits even as we mourn. There exists a sad solidarity, unbidden and perhaps unwanted, among people who are fluent in the language of lament.

I missed a few weeks of services after my dad died. When I returned to work and to the blessed comfort of the prison chapel, that community of brothers supported me as I grieved, more than they may ever know.

Inventions

Whenever the public was permitted to tour the prison, the display that most fascinated laypeople was the assortment of weapons that had been fashioned by inmates and confiscated by the authorities. These were the stabbing implements that inmates invented, either for their own protection or to inflict harm and death on others. The public marveled and shuddered over these weapons, in that very human reaction to gory and gruesome violence: We don't want to see, but we do want to see. The tendency that slows traffic after a bad accident is the same one that prompts us to take a tour of a prison.

The implements of killing were the extreme example of the endless inventiveness of inmates. Necessity being the mother of invention, these men were her natural children, as they had many unmet needs. With so many restrictions on the amount and type of possessions they were allowed, they had figured out how to turn basic supplies into tools and devices and art. By putting books into their net laundry bags, for example, they could still lift weights, because all weight-lifting equipment had been stripped from their recreational options. Using only the precious commodity of toilet tissue and the ink of colored pens, they could create bouquets of flowers. Styrofoam cups and plates were no longer allowed at staff potlucks, because it had been noted that Styrofoam could be melted and shaped and hardened into blades. A spark of fire could be produced in a way that would make Boy Scout leaders proud.

A workable CD player could be rigged from the parts of broken ones. A hot pot's metal plate could produce a righteous grilled cheese sandwich. The most basic food supplies could be turned into a gourmet feast.

The manufacture of alcohol, like the creation of weapons, was a matter of serious contraband. Just about any food with sugar content could be fermented to produce an intoxicating (and I imagine disgusting) beverage known as "pruno." Ingenious inmates who were either alcoholics or entrepreneurs could turn many innocent things into a substance that could get a guy drunk. Pruno required patience and a secret location so the smell didn't give the enterprise away. I once saw officers digging up buckets full of rotting fruit that had been buried near the track. To remove opportunities to ferment things, all sweeteners in prison were artificial, and most fruit was unavailable. Only apples were ubiquitous, included in every box lunch every day. I did see the occasional precious banana.

Smoking was prohibited on all California state property, which applied to staff and inmates. When that law went into effect, the entire prison population by mandate quit on the same day. Or did they? Staff were supposed to leave the prison grounds to smoke on their breaks, but some officers illicitly chewed tobacco on the inside. In an example of ghastly inventiveness, the inmates who were still highly motivated to smoke collected the spit from the chew, dried it out, and smoked it. Apparently an addict's mind, devoid of scruples regarding hygiene, can think up fixes of pure genius.

So another thing I learned from inmates is that nothing is trash. Everything is fixable or recyclable or has a secondary purpose. It occurred to me that my thrifty mother-in-law, who repurposed empty coffee containers and old tissue boxes into crafty gift items, would be at home among these environmentally-conscious inventors.

We staff members assumed that the inmates who collected the trash each day would scrutinize anything we discarded for possible usefulness. We used specially designated "hot trash" receptacles to throw out the things that could be turned into hazardous or dangerous inventions, particularly anything metal, but inmates also collected the hot trash, so I wasn't sure that was an effective procedure.

Once the beaded lanyard that held my ID badge around my neck broke, sending little pink and white beads skittering all over my office floor. Before I could sweep them up and throw them out, which was my intention, Ramon, our Mr. Fix-It, began retrieving them carefully, almost tenderly, in his hand. "Do you have a little bag to put these in?" he asked. "This can be fixed."

I'd intended, of course, to throw the busted lanyard out. I figured it couldn't be restrung to be any stronger than it had been, and I didn't want it to break again, especially because not securing, or worse, *losing* one's badge was a mortal sin in prison. I still had my department-issued, breakaway black lanyard and reattached my badge to it. I'd gotten the pretty beaded one at a teacher supply store. It wasn't expensive. I wouldn't miss it. In my world, it was completely expendable.

But not in Ramon's world. He offered to have one of the beading experts on the yard restring it for me, which I declined. Turning a personal possession over to an inmate was against all the rules, no matter the innocent reason. I thanked him and told him I'd take care of it myself. I took the beads home. I put them in the trash, but not without guilt for my profligate ways.

Inventions on the yard were proof that the human quest to improve the ease and quality of one's life was indefatigable. Along with the ingenuity of these creations, however, I often witnessed a kindness and a generosity among the men that moved me deeply. Like the poor widow in the Gospel of Luke giving the two meager coins she could hardly spare, there were men who offered their last soup or their specific knowledge or even the personal products of their creativity to help a guy out. Along with their clever inventions, these were men reinventing themselves to be of service to their fellows.

Animal Lovers

The library's side window gave me a view of rather a private moment, if there is such a thing in prison. As I was closing and locking up windows for the day, I noticed a lone inmate in an area between buildings where I don't usually see anyone. I stopped my task and felt furtive as I fixated, like an authorized voyeur, on the scene outside the window. I watched him, an older fellow, as he opened a pouch of tuna and tenderly pushed the contents into a plastic bowl for a patient little orange cat. The cat's back legs were pure white, as though she wore the tall vinyl go-go boots of the Sixties or had stepped in a deep bucket of white paint. It made me think of the cat that is mistaken for a female skunk and is relentlessly pursued by Pepe Le Pew after she accidentally acquires a perfectly placed white stripe down her back.

As the orange cat ate, the man gently stroked her fur. I was struck by several thoughts at once, even as I felt like an intruder on this scene of mutual affection. First, a pouch of tuna is expensive for an inmate to purchase. It is available in packages from outside vendors from whom the inmates are only allowed to order once a quarter. It would be a treat for an old man in prison, especially since jobs in prison can top out at 32 cents an hour, and here was this man giving his expensive tuna treasure to a cat. I wondered if a correctional officer would see him and discipline him for noncompliance; it is, of course, against the rules for an inmate to feed any animal. No one bothered him, although I was conscious of two officers out of the corner of my eye going about their business. I was glad to see that, as they say in prison, the officers weren't trippin'. Maybe they were the rare officers who understood that human nature is such that we crave relationships—love and contact and tenderness—if not with other people, then with other living creatures.

I had seen inmates feed and befriend the prison wildlife: squirrels, birds, lizards, spiders. I had noticed them as they gave up their bags of almond snacks and tore up their sandwich bread. Now, this lucky cat. The cats that prowled around the prison were feral, but with persistence and tuna, this one had been won over. The cat allowed her human pal to pet her, and she rubbed her furry length against his trousers when she had finished eating. He bent with old-man difficulty to retrieve the bowl from the ground, but he stayed bent over so that he could pet her for as long as she would have him. I thought about his careful hands, scratching along the cat's sides and under her chin. Whatever those hands had done to someone else to send this man to his term of incarceration, they were peaceful hands now, loving, nonviolent, giving pleasure.

Eventually the man and the cat parted, but in a way that signified that the ritual would be repeated in the future. I didn't know why, but I felt like I had witnessed a holy moment.

Some months later, I'd been around the yard long enough that I adopted my own feral cat. Most of the feral cats around the prison were coarse and mean-looking, but my cat was lithe and elegant. I called her Kitty Carlisle, and only the inmates my age or older knew why. When I was a kid, I watched Kitty Carlisle, an old-time, raven-haired actress, always impeccably dressed and coiffed and bejeweled, on the celebrity panel of the old TV show *To Tell the Truth*. Kitty Carlisle the cat was pure black and sleek. I smuggled in a bag of dry cat food and a small dish, and I fed her in the mornings before the library opened. Almost all of the cats around the prison were fed by other staff members. Some of the officers fed the adorable rabbits and the gangster raccoons. We all broke the rules.

Kitty Carlisle never let me pet her. I was not actually sure that she was a girl. My guess had a 50 percent chance of being right. If I came too close, Kitty Carlisle got skittish and ran for shelter under the rosebushes in the courtyard. Still, I heard her meowing by the door in the morning, and I knew she had learned our routine.

Prison, of course, is all about routine, the procedures for how things run set in stone, the course of each day largely unchanging. Unlike prison in Hollywood, real prison is stultifyingly boring. When an inmate is released, he often has trouble adjusting to the variety of everything out there, and the unpredictability of life on the outside. He is not accustomed to making the thousands of daily decisions that we take for granted as part of the deal of living.

But routine can serve us well in life on the outside, especially if we are pet owners. The main reason I take a walk every evening around six p.m. is that my dog demands it. He waits by the door. If I tarry, he nags me. He is geriatric, but he wants that walk, rain or shine or wind or fog. And then dinner.

Many of us, even non-pet owners, function best when we have a daily rhythm, and certainly family life is built on a foundation of routine and habit and tradition. It's comforting to know what the day has in store for us; it's soothing to respond to a set of daily expectations and purposes. It's just that prison takes routine to its extreme, and extremes are usually not healthy.

Cat Lessons

A feral kitten joined our family after he'd been separated from his mother. It turned out that Kitty Carlisle was in fact female, and although she was prolific, she was not especially maternal. I thought the kitten would be better off with us in our home. I came to doubt this.

The kitten had gotten lost near the vocational classrooms behind the education department. Leo, the inmate maintenance worker who heard the kitten crying on a summer day and rescued him from under a pile of old pipes and lumber, was forbidden to keep him. He brought him to the library in a box. Maybe six weeks old, the kitten was black, with a wee spot of white on his chest. He definitely favored his mother, and Lord knows if his father was some sort of incestuous relation to her. Back at home, our beloved cat had met an untimely death in the jaws of a neighbor's dog two years earlier, so I thought my husband might be ready for a kitten. My husband is the cat person in the family.

"I guess the universe has spoken," he said. I brought the kitten home. Now he was ours.

Or was he?

My husband named him Dewey, honoring his library roots, which seemed original until I came across a whole book titled *Dewey*, about a cat that had been abandoned in a book drop in winter and lived the rest of his life in a warm public library. So maybe not so original.

Leo occasionally stopped by the library to ask how Dewey was getting on, like a parent who'd given up his child for adoption. I knew it had pained him not to keep the kitten. I brought in a photo of Dewey climbing on a carpeted cat tree. Leo showed up in the library a few months later with a timid gray kitten in a box. "Look, Ms. Schultz, it's a little girl," he said. I confess that I was relieved when one of the vocational instructors stepped up and took her home. Although my husband would have liked it, I wasn't keen to establish the official home for feral prison cats.

As Dewey grew, and as he approached his first birthday, I realized that he was a textbook study of the "nature v. nurture" debate. For example, because of the neighbor's aforementioned hound, we kept Dewey indoors. But even though he was a baby when he joined our family and shouldn't really know any better than the confines of the house, he longed to be outdoors. We provided him with cat toys of every hue and sound, yet he tired of them quickly. He disdained them, really. We fed him high-quality cat food, yet he sat by the window and followed the movement of birds in the trees with hunger in his eyes.

Dewey showed me that, although we thought we could tame him, he would remain untamed. He came from a long line of felines who survived outdoors on little more than their wits and hunting skills. We had given him everything he needed, but it seemed he would rather be fending for himself. We had loved him unconditionally, but he remained unallied. He wanted to be near us all the time, maybe to keep an eye on what we were up to, but he did not know how to accept our affection. When we petted him, he bit us. When we snuggled him, he scratched us. Although he slept on our bed at night, by day he was unapproachable.

So after another few months, we got him his rabies shot. Then we let him venture outside, little by little, to explore and mark territory and even hunt stuff. He reminded me of something I had to learn as a parent: that children are better off when we don't give them everything they desire, when they have to work out solutions to problems on their own, try different approaches to overcome obstacles, and even fail at some endeavors. The process of life forms us as we risk growing.

Perhaps people are by nature like cats: we have to challenge our wits and skills in order to hone them and to grasp for our full potential. We have to follow our genuine instincts and fulfill who we are, lest we grow soft and lazy. And we have to honor each other for who we are. Dewey needs to be free, to feel the dirt under his paws and the sun warming his black fur and the breeze on his little cat face. It's who he is.

Flies for Henrietta

Earl found a solution for the annoying flies in the library when he inherited a pet lizard from a dorm-mate who paroled. The lizard had been named Henry, but an expert herpetologist on the yard corrected her gender identification, and thus her name, to Henrietta.

Henrietta came to work with Earl every day. He constructed a lizard condominium for her from an old packing box. It reminded me of the dioramas kids made for school projects, portraying the land of the dinosaurs or the Battle of Waterloo in a decorated shoebox. He kept the box behind the counter, next to the books that needed repair. Mostly, though, Henrietta lived inside Earl's shirt.

"She likes to be warm," Earl said.

And she liked to eat live insects. Henrietta grew fat on the flies that Earl captured for her in the library. Earl developed a patented method for catching the hapless flies in a plastic bag without quite killing them. I'd see him cupping his quarry on a wall or a window, bag covering his hand, satisfaction on his face.

"She likes them alive," Earl said.

A previous clerk, Anton, had sometimes brought his lizard to the library for safekeeping, especially whenever the officers were conducting a search of his dorm. I always told him to take the lizard back to his bunk at night, however, in case the yard went on lockdown. Lockdown meant that there was no movement on the yard except for medical or security reasons. The library was closed. Inmates could request materials in writing, but they could not physically come to the library. During lockdown, I usually organized and cataloged and cleaned everything I could think of. Lockdowns made me realize how much I enjoyed the human interaction that came with my job. The hours of lockdown days dragged. The library was peaceful and quiet, but it was unused, which seemed a sorry state for a library. Its purpose was thwarted, as nothing was being read or used or browsed or consulted. It was a still life. If the phone rang, I jumped.

On day 3 of one particular lockdown, I passed by the plastic US postal bin that Anton kept his lizard in while he was at work in the library, and I saw movement in the high desert habitat.

Anton's lizard. He (she?) was so good at camouflage that he had been hiding in there for three days, and I hadn't detected him. Crap, I thought. The lizard must be hungry and thirsty. I considered setting him free, but what if he was too tame to survive? And would I break Anton's heart if I let his pet go? The lizard's well-being was up to me for the duration of the lockdown, and I didn't want the lizard on my conscience.

So I decided the lizard, whom I had taken to calling Eddie Izzard in my loneliness, was not going to die on my watch. I poured water in the little cup I used to water my plants and set it in Eddie Izzard's US postal bin domain. I gave him a few bamboo leaves from my plant, even though I knew Eddie was no vegetarian. Since I was, my lunch was of no use. I needed insects. I needed flies.

I gave Eddie the few dead things I found on the windowsills, but I knew he required fresh kills, or even live prey. Against all my principles, I became a hunter. I killed two flies. I trapped a spider. I rationalized that Eddie had to eat. I offered him the bounty of the hunt. I considered going to the pet store and buying crickets but wasn't sure if crickets would be considered contraband. Eddie's fate was in my unwilling hands, but I didn't want to lose my job because of some crickets. But I did feel less alone in Eddie's company. I didn't want him to die. I stayed on the lookout for flies.

The lockdown fortunately ended the next day, and Eddie Izzard survived my care. But I told Anton never to leave his pets overnight again. My heart couldn't take the responsibility.

So Earl knew never to leave Henrietta overnight, but she was a daily fixture. Other inmates brought Earl the random bugs they'd come across and watched with fascination as Henrietta consumed her prey. Henrietta was a pretty pampered lizard. She was a blue-bellied something or other, native to our area. She was also completely against the rules, as Eddie

Izzard had been, as all animals in an inmate's possession were. Since Henrietta had lived her whole life in captivity, however, it seemed cruel to send her back into the wild of the dusty prison yard.

One day Earl came to work in a foul mood. He was meaner than usual to the library patrons and seemed like he was itching to start a fight with somebody. I called him into my office so that he could catch the big fat fly that was buzzing around, but really to ask him what his deal was.

He turned away so I wouldn't see his mouth trembling. Earl was trying not to cry. EARL. Tears filled the eyes of the toughest mo-fo on the yard.

"I killed Henrietta," he said.

Somehow—I didn't quite get how, but the details seemed unimportant—Earl had not realized that Henrietta was hanging out on his back, and when he had either sat down too hard or leaned or fallen or *something*, Henrietta was smushed to death. I could see that Earl's heart was broken in two, but also that he thought he was the most worthless jerk in the world. He had finally loved someone, and he had taken her life. He could do nothing right.

I said words of comfort—who knows what platitudes—as he wiped his face. I told him to take the rest of the day off: bereavement leave seemed in order, because Earl was in mourning.

I too grieved for his loss, because Earl had opened himself up to love another creature after so many years of solitude, and he was not likely to do so again anytime soon. Love hurts, I wanted to say. But love makes you see God reflected in unlikely places, even in yourself. Don't stop loving, I wanted to say. But I didn't.

He paused in the doorway on his way out.

"Don't need no more flies," he said. The low, sad, heartbroken way he said it made my heart crumple, too.

Naturalists on the Yard

Something we humans on the outside have lost, with the advent of handheld technology, is the ability to observe nature. I got a first-hand glimpse of this phenomenon when I took a road trip with my sister and two nephews, ages ten and eight. As we drove hundreds of miles across these United States, I witnessed my sister's brave struggle to limit the boys' screen time on their devices and instead encourage them to look out the car windows.

"Look at that river/mountain/bridge/train/old barn/herd of sheep!" my sister would call.

"Yeah," the boys would reply, looking up briefly to placate her, before returning to their current game obsession. A river was no match for the virtual hunt.

In prison, there were few distractions. Technology was just beginning to come to the yard in the form of CDCR-approved tablets, which could be loaded with music and games, but the tablets were expensive and unreliable. Many inmates had not had any interaction with the technology revolution that gripped the rest of us. "Do you know," a lifer once asked me in wonder, "that on the outside there are whole stores that only sell *phones*?" I did know that: I dreaded having to visit one of them. He just couldn't imagine the point of such a place.

If young people ever want to study what the world was like before cell phones, they could check out prison culture.

In their free time away from jobs or school, inmates were likely to play cards or chess on handmade sets, or read or watch TV or work out or walk the track or write letters or shoot the breeze, just to make the idle hours pass. A good number of men became close observers of nature. Just like it could be on the outside, nature lent itself to occasions for reflection and serenity. Since the prison was located ten miles outside the nearest town, wildlife abounded. There were raccoons, mice, chipmunks, squirrels, snakes, lizards, feral cats, and birds of every feather. The naturalists could tell the difference between a crow and a raven just by their call. They could determine the sex of a lizard. They followed the cycles of the new generations of baby animals. They shared (surreptitiously) their little bags of almonds with the squirrels. They noted changes in clouds and foliage, winds and temperature. They watched the risings and settings of sun, moon, and stars. They anticipated the changing of the seasons. They were simply aware of and attuned to nature in a way that many of us on the outside no longer are.

Nature afforded them a brief respite from the close quarters and noise and controlled chaos of dorm living. Sitting outside under the sky or walking the innumerable laps around the track that many of them walked every day, perhaps a man could forget for a moment that he was caged, that while his body was confined to the legal parameters of the prison, his spirit could still soar. Perhaps fresh air smelled like freedom. Perhaps the feel of sun on skin was a tiny escape. "[God] makes his sun rise on the bad and the good, and causes rain to fall on the just and the unjust," wrote Matthew in his gospel (5:45), a truth that did not go unnoticed in prison.

One of the library patrons had actually been a meteorologist on the outside. He asked if he could write up short analyses of the weather for our quarterly newsletter for the yard. My favorite title, for a piece he wrote on the patterns of precipitation that we could expect one winter, was "El Niño or El

No-no?" He requested that I print out the monthly update that was available on the NOAA (National Oceanic and Atmospheric Administration, a federal agency) website. I did so, even though he was the only person I knew who could understand its complex charts and syntax. To make my life easier, I had signed up for the NOAA's automatic monthly emails. After the meteorologist transferred to another prison, I felt a pang of sadness every month when that NOAA update arrived in my inbox. I should have cancelled it, but I didn't.

To paraphrase a famous saying, some naturalists are born, some are trained, and some have nature thrust upon them. The yard naturalists were mostly in that last category, adjusting to yet another consequence thrust upon them.

Or Lack Thereof

The fabulous state of California has birthed so many technological innovations that one would think that the state government would have top-of-the-line technology in place in all departments. After all, we are the home of Silicon Valley. Oddly, the state prison system's technology was located in the Forgotten-by-Time Valley. For example, when I first worked in Records, a supervisor directed me to finish filling out a sex registration form for a paroling sex offender, to be filed with the state Department of Justice and the police department having jurisdiction in his prospective city. The inmate had signed the bottom of the form and affixed his thumbprint, but the information lines on the original form were blank.

"How do I do that?" I asked.

She pointed to something under a draped cover on a small table in the back of the office. "On that," she said.

I lifted the cover to find a typewriter.

"Don't make any mistakes," she said. "You can't use white-out on the original."

I was momentarily speechless. A typewriter. An electric typewriter, like the kind I hadn't used since typing research papers in college in the 1970s.

"You're kidding, right?" I finally said, but she had already walked away.

Everything in the inmates' central files was on paper. Every important document or report was a hard copy. This was in

2008, when the rest of the country had pretty much digitized all kinds of files. It would be another four years before the California Department of Corrections and Rehabilitation began to establish a comprehensive system of online central files and an offender tracking system, and to train us on how to implement these new programs. The upside, when this revolution finally happened, was that we were joining the twenty-first century. The downside was that many clerical employees in the Records office were laid off or reassigned, including me. Less paper meant less need for filing hands.

So when I started in the prison library, I was less surprised to see typewriters in use than I might otherwise have been had I not recently had to use one myself. These technological dinosaurs were the only means for inmates to produce a court document that looked even slightly professional. The courts were fully aware of the scarce resources available to inmates, and so handwritten documents were perfectly acceptable. It was rumored that the landmark *Miranda* case, the famous one that required police to inform anyone being arrested of their legal rights, had been submitted to the court on toilet paper. As long as a court clerk could read a submission, and as long as it adhered to the rules of the court, it was acceptable.

Only the most eccentric writers in the outside world still used a typewriter, but in the library, the typewriters were in constant use. The three typewriters we had were precious. We had a fourth one in the back that we raided for parts. In my early days in the library, I had sent a fifth one to the maintenance shop to be repaired, but it never came back. When I inquired about its progress, I was told that I had never turned in a work order for a typewriter, or a typewriter, for that matter. I had, but there was no use arguing. The typewriter had vanished. The important lesson I learned was never to surrender another irreplaceable machine into the black hole of the maintenance department. Besides, one of my clerks—Ramon, a.k.a. MacGyver—was able to put together a sort of Frankenstein typewriter out of spare parts.

Our typewriters were also missing some helpful features, like the long metal bar that held the paper on the roller and kept the paper from slipping out of alignment. These thin metal bars had been deemed "weapon stock," which meant that engineering inmates could use them to create lethal stabbing weapons, a definite threat to the safety and security of the institution, and so they had all been removed and confiscated. It was always comforting to limit the raw materials that could be used to take you out, but the lack of those guiding bars made for some uneven lines of typing.

The consumable supplies—ribbon cartridges and correction tape wheels and print wheels—were also hard to come by. I ordered them every month from the supply warehouse but didn't always receive what I ordered. Sometimes I received typewriter supplies from different manufacturers that were incompatible with the models we had, but those were useful in the unofficial barter system on the yard. I could sometimes trade with the clerks in the kitchen or the program office, because every area that employed inmate workers was still using typewriters. When you worked in the prison, you took a step back through several decades of technological progress when you arrived for work every morning. The inmates lived there permanently.

The other technology issue affecting the smooth operation of the library was that all the library records were also on paper. We did checkouts and inventories by hand. This was a good way to maintain wildly inaccurate records, of course, and the monthly report that I was required to do was largely fictional. Other prison libraries around the state were already on the second generation of electronic checkout systems, but ours was still in the Dark Ages. We were a bit embarrassed when we went to statewide training sessions and had to admit that we still had not implemented the first approved electronic system. We did have those adjustable date stamps for the due dates in the books, but that was the height of our library technology. During my last year there, we finally got the hardware and the software to create a digital inventory and to put in place a computerized checkout system. This meant we could also track our books, and even put them on reserve, just like a real library. It may seem like a small accomplishment, but we felt like we'd won gold in the Library Olympics. We could print reports and overdue notices. Our monthly numbers were no longer fictitious but were backed up by verifiable electronic data. The clerks got hands-on experience in computer input and scanning, although this only came after a long fight with the institutional powers to allow inmates to touch the computer. Technology was opening a Pandora's box of security issues, but it was coming. It was long overdue.

College Comes to Prison

When I started working at the library, inmates could only take college classes through the mail. The snail mail. Several community colleges offered programs specifically for people who would never be able to come to their campus. These colleges designed courses that could be completed in writing, even including labs. The state provided fee waivers for enrollment, and indigent students could borrow the textbooks that we kept in the library for each course. They were supposed to purchase a course outline that contained the syllabus and assignments, but these were available online and could be printed and copied by me. Most often, inmates finished their education by earning an associate's degree. The rare ones with money, of course, could pursue all the higher degrees they could afford, but these programs were also possible to complete only through correspondence courses.

But thanks to a federal court order to reduce the prison population, the state of California began a real push to honor the *R* in CDCR and actually put some funding into rehabilitative programs. A face-to-face college program was established in every state prison. This meant that a nearby community college brought real classes with real live professors to our yard.

The excitement for these classes to begin was palpable. The lifers on the yard were especially pleased to be able to add educational accomplishments to their potential parole presentations. The library, along with its resources, became important to students who had to complete research papers or prepare oral reports. Academic needs began to take over more of our library space.

The limitations to these new classes were apparent right away: the inmates had no access to the internet, where college students normally do their research. They could request information from their professors, who then printed out pertinent articles or references and brought them in with them, but the students weren't actually learning how to do research in this brave new world that had left them behind. Our *World Book Encyclopedia* was not going to meet college-level research needs. The library already had a system in place whereby an inmate could fill out an information request slip for such things as a helpful organization's address or a fact or statistic easily retrievable from Wikipedia—nothing personal like a baby mama's whereabouts, although that had been asked—but I had neither the time nor the directive to fulfill more complicated college-related demands. The students also had to handwrite their term papers; lacking computers and printers, they had no way to use word-processing technology. Those who had personal typewriters could type their work, of course, but no matter how hard they tried, the end results always looked smeary and unprofessional. Imagine having to follow APA format with a ballpoint pen.

The professors had to learn, like any new staffers in prison, how to teach and be helpful and personable without being subject to manipulation. They also had a tough time adjusting to the fact that, even if they had driven many miles and had a class planned according to their syllabus, the safety and security of the institution trumped their program. And every other program. If there was a yard recall, or a lockdown, the custody staff did not care about the impeded progress of a college course. The face-to-face college program lacked one obvious advantage of the correspondence course, which was that the timetable was not subject to the reality of a day in prison gone awry: correspondence students worked at their own pace and in their own space.

All the same, it was lovely to watch inmates who perhaps hadn't finished high school on the outside become serious college students, who complained about their workloads, who diligently read their chapters so they could participate in class discussions, who bought yellow highlighters with their meager funds, who sweated out their grade on their latest paper or exam. They compared notes on professors and made outlines for studying together. They didn't exactly look like college students; they were too old, too world-weary, too hardened by their graduation from the school of the street. But they acted like college students. Their minds were expanding. Their mindsets were upending. They were getting educated.

Best of all, the prison education department sponsored periodic graduation ceremonies. Inmates could graduate from several areas: they could earn their GED diplomas or vocational program certifications or college degrees. The ceremony was dignified by an official printed program, borrowed caps and gowns, the presence of dignitaries like the warden and invited guests like family members of the inmates, inspirational speeches by the graduates, live music from the inmate band, and colorful decorations, and it was all topped off by the rare delights of punch and cake and ice cream. Graduation Day was magical in that it was a glimmer of normal life come alive within the confines of the visiting room. It was always fascinating to meet the mothers and grandmothers and spouses and children of men I knew as single entities. It was heartening to know that the men I cared about were loved and supported by their families. And it was heartbreaking to see the ones who had no guests to invite.

College classes quickly became a reality and a staple. My hope is that college programs and other rehabilitative programs will continue to expand until they become an expected part of prison offerings. The tax dollars spent on rehabilitation will be repaid by improvements in public safety and human dignity.

My Alarm

My staff alarm was a little grubby. The plastic back that held in the battery was gone, and some enterprising officer had fixed it with duct tape. Because that's how you fix everything. The tape had since begun to curl and decompose around the edges, possibly from stuffing it in and out of my pocket every day. Its appearance was a little embarrassing.

My alarm was technically referred to as a Personal Alarm Device, or PAD, because the lingo rules of the department dictated that one always used 66 percent more words than one actually needed, and a snappy acronym for those words was always preferable. Most of us still referred to our PAD as our alarm.

Because that's what it was, pure and simple. If I, as free staff, was alarmed by anything I encountered in the course of the day, I was supposed to push the button on my alarm to summon custody staff to my area. My alarm looked like an old-fashioned garage door opener. A tiny glow of a red light let me know that my alarm was indeed in working order. It was also tested every day, after I went home. I carried my alarm everywhere. Free staff were encouraged to purchase utility belts that have multiple nooks and hooks for equipment such as alarms and keys, but I resisted, for several reasons: I was neither an officer nor Batman, I did not look good in belts, and said utility belt was expensive. Instead, I invested in several pairs of cargo pants, which were a kind of uniform for me. My alarm fit snugly and reassuringly along my right leg, and my keys were in my hip pocket. Some people left their alarms in a desk drawer or briefcase, which was a super bad idea in prison. You never knew when a benign situation might turn malignant.

Free staff also had to carry a Department-issue whistle, in case you were away from the designated area of your alarm or your alarm didn't work. Your whistle was kept with your department badge on a lanyard around your neck, which was of a breakaway design so an inmate couldn't choke you with your own equipment. The Department thought of everything.

In fourteen or so years of my time in prison, first as a volunteer and then as an employee, I hit my alarm exactly twice. The first time was on the occasion of a fistfight outside the library door, which I happened upon when I was about to close the door for a staff meeting. The second time was when a library patron attempted to pleasure himself under the cover of a library table. It was considered a kind of free-staff-baptism to hit your alarm by accident, but I never did. Triggering a false alarm was mortifying, because when an alarm went off on the yard, all inmates were required to drop to the ground, and all available custody staff ran flat out to the source of the alarm, expecting serious trouble. If you caused an alarm by mistake, it was a special kind of shame. The false-alarmer was unofficially expected to bring donuts to the diligent responders the next day.

I saw custody staff responding with less alacrity when the alarming area was prone to accidental pushes. The two responses to my alarms happened with great speed, as the library had a reputation of not initiating alarms. The people in green figured it was really serious if it was coming from the library. I admit that I was proud of this rep. Short of the aforementioned outright physical violence or inappropriate bliss, we handled our own issues in the library.

Knowing when to hit your alarm could be tricky. If you didn't hit it immediately and tried to manage a situation by yourself, a sergeant was sure to ask you, "Why the hell didn't you hit your alarm?" If you did hit your alarm, and it turned out that your life was not in jeopardy, some other sergeant would ask you, "Why the hell did you hit your alarm?" The exact correct time to hit your alarm was a mystery. We were told to hit it first and ask questions later, but the questions-later part could be unpleasant.

I loved my alarm. It made me feel safe, and indeed I was safer than if I'd worked in a public library or a school library. I knew there were no automatic weapons coming through my door. And I knew that if something crazy happened, help was just a footrace away. Sometimes I wished that I had an alarm in my daily life. Having to dial 9-1-1, then waiting for an answer, and then having to explain my emergency seemed much more difficult than pressing a button. In prison, the response came first and the questions and paperwork later.

And of course, this being the Department, there was paperwork for everyone after an alarm sounded. The paperwork was mostly digital, as the incident reporting was done online, but forms are still forms, and lingo is still lingo. A report may have gone through several rewrites to get it right, and precise, technical language was required. For example, you could not say, "Inmate X was pleasuring himself." You had to elaborate: "Inmate X had his right hand under the table, inside his pants, and he was moving it repeatedly in an up-and-down motion." Get the picture? In reports, the precision of every word mattered.

I was not supposed to keep personal items in my work area on the yard, but my alarm felt like my most personal possession. It was my companion, my reminder of where I worked, and my security blanket. Like the Department, it was grubby, it was in disrepair, but it was a part of me.

The Regulars

One way not to go nuts while in captivity was to hang out at the library. The library offered not only books and magazines to read, but the kind of people who read things and thought about things and had opinions about things. The kind of people who were interested in not being knuckleheads. So the library had a group of patrons whom I thought of as the regulars, from the ones who spent many hours in the library to the ones who were voracious readers and always needed fresh reading material to the ones who just popped in every day to say hello.

The regulars were usually settled in their seats again on Tuesday—or as one regular specifically put it, "the last seat in the corner by the Business section"—after another busy Monday in the library. Mondays were awash in a rush of inmates who had stewed all weekend in their need for legal copies or the next volume of a particular fantasy series or to check on the status of some rumor they'd heard on Saturday during visiting. On Mondays we quickly reached our maximum capacity of fifty patrons, so we had to hustle people in and out to keep the line outside under control. On busy days we logged over three hundred walk-ins. By Tuesday, things were usually back to normal. The regulars could rest easy.

The seriously insatiable readers among the regulars visited the library daily. They read their way through the shelves. Reading was a reliable mental escape. Even men who came to prison functionally illiterate often became quite well-read over their years of incarceration just through seeking relief from the boredom. One sci-fi lover liked to read the science fiction books that were written in the 1950s and hadn't been checked out since. He delighted in reading me the blurbs about a future—say, the year 2000—envisioned by an author who got it all wrong. Another reader had a really nice mom who regularly sent him the latest books in a popular series. He was kind enough to donate these precious gems once he'd read them.

Most of the regulars were indeed pretty regular: guys who were working on their legal cases or their studies, or who liked to read or write letters in the calm of the library. Some, however, were quirkier and therefore more memorable.

There was the newspaper-reader, a guy who read the same papers over and over, outdated copies of *The Los Angeles Times* and *USA Today*. He pored over weeks-old news and sometimes tore out pertinent bits of newsprint, which was against the rules. I made him sit up front, since I'd never been able to catch him red-handed.

There was the fellow with the stack of ragged papers two feet high, copies of litigation that somehow had not yet earned him the designation of "Vexatious Litigant" from the court in which he filed his incessant motions. (When courts deemed a petitioner so, it meant that the frivolity of his submissions got him banned from filing anything with that particular court for a designated period of time. It also meant that I didn't have to put up with his nonsense, either.) He was a conspiracy theorist, going so far as to try to demonstrate that everything the court sent him, down to the name of the court clerk, was written in a secret code he'd cracked that actually spelled out ominous things like "SILENCE HIM AT ONCE." The court, to its credit, was still taking his motions seriously, even though it denied every single one of them.

There was the gay couple who spent tons of time in the library, but who never checked out any books. They sat close together, deep in conversation, but also aware of the watchful eyes of the clerks who disapproved of the relationship. I kept an eye on them, too, because I didn't want the library to gain a reputation as a place you could go to get intimate, but I also welcomed them as a lesson in tolerance for some of the homophobic patrons. Their information requests helped me add to our LGBTQ reference materials, of which we started out with very few.

There was the Spanish-speaking group of men who met weekly to get help with their math skills, so they could pass that section of the GED exam. I sometimes had to ask Gus, their bilingual tutor, to keep his voice down, as he got excited in his quest to bring about an understanding of decimals and fractions. Gus had the heart of a teacher. "You missed your calling," I told him. He got a little teary. Which got me a little teary.

Funny story: One day I heard an inmate yelling insults at Gus, who managed to calm the guy down. The same inmate then tried to start a verbal altercation with me. I told him to leave the library. It turned out that this inmate had been trying to get himself in trouble and sent to Ad-Seg, because he owed a debt to some serious dudes on the yard. "That guy tried to provoke the two calmest people on the yard," Gus said. We laughed like crazy, but I knew Gus was proud of his newfound self-restraint.

There was the frail old man who adored *Bartlett's Familiar Quotations*. Since that was a reference volume, he could not check it out and bring it back to his dorm like a dear friend, which is what he would have liked to do. Instead, he requested it every day and made slow progress through its pages at the Reference Table, reading it as though it were a novel, cover to cover. He often copied down a pleasing quote and then shared it with me. He was a lefty.

There was the weaselly guy whose elder abuse had resulted in his father's death. Now there was estate money involved, and he had the gall to spend hours in the library researching how to fight his siblings for his share. The deep circles under his eyes made him look like he was regularly punched, and at first I felt sorry for him, even though he treated me, along with all the library clerks, like the hired help. Earl would have liked to punch him. I confess that after enduring many months of his complaints about the rudeness of my clerks and his evaluations of my own inefficiency as his personal library slave, I kind of wanted to punch him, too. He was also a lefty.

I noticed a high percentage of left-handed people in the library. I don't have actual numbers for an empirical study, but as I am a lefty, I always notice when other people are as well. I feel a kinship with them. Lefties have always seemed to me like a big extended family, like something out of a Vonnegut novel. We all know from an early age that we are different— weird, odd ducks, misfits in a right-handed world—so it makes some sense that prison would be full of people like us. Many of the regulars were lefties.

The library gradually added features to help alleviate the slow monotony of prison life. Everything in the waiting room called prison was slow: slow technology, slow access to news, and slow legal machinations all made for slow days that begged for something, *anything,* different. Inspired by a statewide training for library workers, I introduced a self-help book report program. If an inmate read five self-help books from the library and completed a two-page book report form, he was given a certificate and a "chrono," which was an official form in his central file that commended his accomplishment. The lifers especially benefitted from accruing chronos in their files, as chronos furnished the parole board with checkable proof of participation in rehabilitative programs. I brought in some old jigsaw puzzles, which kept some heads that might otherwise have been arguing bent closely together in concentration. The puzzle table was addictive, and the addicts included me. We handed out free copies of crossword puzzles, sudokus, and word searches.

In honor of the very fine artists on the yard, the senior librarian instituted thematic art contests and awarded prizes, usually cans of diet soda donated by the recreational teacher, whom everyone called "Coach." We tried to get permission to paint a mural on the soaring library walls but did not succeed. We printed and distributed bookmarks with designs that had been submitted in a bookmark contest. One of my coworkers started an art group, with the goal of exploring the different artistic media practiced by the many experts on the yard, such as drawing, painting, and beading. She was a knitter, so we used library funds to purchase some starter knitting kits. Soon she had a group of eight or so inmates knitting away, some more successfully than others. One of my favorite sights in the library was a group of hardened criminals sitting around a library table, chatting and knitting and comparing stitches like a bunch of grandmas.

I do miss those regulars. I'm hoping they remember that there are libraries on the outside, too, ready to offer resources and opportunities and even community and encouragement when they need them.

The Rumor Mill

Every workplace has its drama. I remember thinking, when I took a job at a Catholic parish, that my workplace would be spiritual and tranquil. Surely it would be quite different from secular workplaces. This was far from the truth. Even with a crucifix in every room, the church workplace was no more holy than other workplaces, with the same gossip, mis-understandings, close quarters, personality conflicts, resent-ments, and rumors.

Prison is no different, except that my coworkers were mostly inmates, with whom I had to walk the fine line between ca-maraderie and over-familiarity. Over-familiarity is the great sin of prison staff. We were not permitted to share personal details or food or physical contact (even a handshake) or any suggestion of being equals with inmates. We were to keep all inmates at arm's length—literally, you hold your arm out straight to measure your inviolable personal space—and keep social interaction to a minimum.

This is mostly impossible. Of course you develop relation-ships with the people with whom you work side-by-side seven hours a day. Some staff members do manage to keep a tight and formal distance, but they are sometimes the ones who refer to inmates as "animals" or "apes" or even "cockroaches." This approach guaranteed them an emotional distance based on their own sense of superiority.

Having begun my time in prison as a religious volunteer, I regularly shook hands with inmates. When I came back to those Communion services after my dad died, an inmate who had also lost his father hugged me. The spontaneous gesture caught us both off guard, but I did not report it. I was grateful for the comfort from another grieving child.

But one of the harder things to keep a lid on in prison is the 24/7, never-closed rumor mill. There are a couple reasons for the rampant rumors in prison. First, you have an idle population, at least the inmates who are not in school or employed or in any way interested in self-help work. These guys sometimes spread outlandish rumors just for fun. They alleviate their tedium by watching the outraged reactions to whatever news they have just fabricated. Then you have a lack of hard information. Except for television, nothing is instant in prison. Newspapers and letters are late, opportunities for phone calls are unreliable or too expensive, and the immediacy of the internet is absent.

The library, being a source of information, was often the first place an inmate came to verify the latest wild thing he'd heard. For example, was there really going to be a mass release of inmates due to overcrowded prison conditions? And was this going to happen by the end of this week? "My girlfriend saw it online," they'd say. They'd accuse me of covering up a scoop or withholding positive information if I couldn't locate the same information on my computer, which I'd try to do and come up empty. After several of these attempts, I had a better idea.

"On your next phone call, have your girlfriend spell the website," I'd say. "Otherwise, I can't find anything like this thing she told you."

One memorable rumor concerned something that had happened in the Vocational Welding classroom. An inmate had tried to lift some nefariously unwieldy piece of equipment by himself, which student welders are apparently never supposed to do, and then dropped it. The equipment had severed both of his big toes, right through his sturdy prison-issue boots. "It was just like a guillotine!" came the breathless report. I felt a little sick, imagining the blood and the poor toes and the welding instructor's horror. Could you sew toes back on? Did someone retrieve them and send them along with the student to Medical? Speculation was that the toes were surely too dead to be reattached by the time they got delivered to an outside hospital.

When I asked the instructor about this gruesome tale, he shook his head. Then he told me the real thing that happened was that the inmate had broken a couple of toes. They'd been taped.

Another time, I came to work on a Monday morning and heard that, over the weekend, a line of black SUVs had arrived at the prison and had taken the warden away in handcuffs. "In cuffs!" the rumormongers chortled. Since the warden was named personally in every civil lawsuit any inmate ever filed against the Department, ill fortune befalling the warden was a perennial rumor.

Of course, the warden was safe at work in the warden's office, unaffected by any such drama.

One afternoon, an inmate stopped to talk to me on his way out of the library.

"Sorry to hear you're leaving," he said.

Hmm. Did he know something I didn't know? No, he had simply put two and two together and come up with something other than four. He had noticed that the newly-hired librarian had been sharing my office while her permanent location was still being decided. Because she was much younger than I, the inmate concluded that I was obviously training my replacement. Suddenly, my imminent departure was all over the yard. Strangely, I had been mulling over the possibility of retiring but hadn't told anyone. His best wishes caught me off guard. I didn't actually retire for another year and a half.

The concurrent rumor to this one was that the new librarian was actually my daughter. This, too, was untrue.

Rumors in any environment can cause hard feelings and, worse, the destruction of reputations. In prison there is also the threat of physical harm resulting from a false rumor. Particularly serious were rumors that involved a bogus report of an inmate's commitment offense. Crimes involving children and/or sex offenses relegated an inmate to the bottom rung of the prison social ladder, so many inmates kept the details of their crimes as private as possible. But a middle-aged white guy with no gang affiliation or priors was assumed to be a child molester. For him, a rumor could bring violent repercussions.

One sad result of a rumor involved old man Wilson, a lifer in his late seventies. Some inmates got hold of a parole report from Records that listed upcoming parole dates for inmates on the yard. Wilson's date was listed within the week. Wilson came into the library to say goodbye to me, beaming rays of sunshine at his good fortune. Having worked in Records, I suspected that the date was Wilson's eligibility date for a hearing with the parole board, not an actual physical release date, as both kinds of dates were noted on that particular report.

"I can't believe this is happening," Wilson said. "The good Lord has plans for me of which I know naught." Wilson, like many inmates, was an amateur biblical scholar.

"You should check with your counselor," I told him. "It may be different from what you think."

Wilson wasn't about to let the library lady rain on his parade.

"The fellas in R & R saw the list!" he said, a little testy. "I'm on it!" Receiving and Release controlled every inmate who went in or out of the prison. Unfortunately, the fellas (inmates) who worked there did not know how to read the columns of codes on the list. Wilson was not going anywhere without a hearing.

Until his date came and went, however, Wilson continued to plan his first meal of freedom and to bid adieu to his dorm mates. He gave stuff away. He walked on air. And then he didn't.

The next time I saw Wilson, he had aged ten years and walked in a fog of unshakeable despondency. I'd been right about the report, but I still felt crappy about it. Rumors can ruin a man.

Tattoos

Oh, they were everywhere. They carpeted the skin. They were sometimes beautiful and sometimes brutal.

Tattoo art is as old as the ancient marks found on mummies and as new as this morning. They have been used to indicate rank and identify criminals for life and brand the innocent victims of concentration camps. They have been paraded in freak shows and immortalized by the Marx Brothers on the dazzling skin of "Lydia, oh Lydia, that encyclo-pydia."

Random tattoos I spotted on my patrons: A hand grenade below the ear. A woman's name—many women's names—on a collarbone. Rosaries and crucifixes and Bible verses. Gang symbols. The Virgin of Guadalupe. Faces of dead friends. Place names and maps. A faint mustache where you'd think one would grow anyway. A phrase on the side of a shaved head: "F*ck what you think."

"You don't even know what I think," I said to this last guy, when he arrived for the first time in the library. He looked puzzled and then sheepish as he realized what I'd just read on the side of the bald head that was facing me. At least he'd be able to join the group of men I'd noticed who had started to let their hair grow in, so they could cover up offensive words or images before a parole hearing or an actual release date. Or he might find that the hair he was counting on was no longer a possibility, that the shining baldness he thought he'd chosen was now, thanks to the inevitable aging process, a *fait accompli*.

Tattoos no longer faze me, in prison or in public. My daughters all have tattoos, which members of their generation seem to view as innocuous but permanent jewelry. I had to overcome my initial horror at seeing their beautiful skin, God-given and nurtured by me from the time of their birth, forever defaced by the whims of style. Their tattoos may be art, but I don't have to appreciate them. The tattoos my daughters have chosen, fortunately, are delicate and very colorful, unlike the dull inking that gets done on the down low in prison. Tattoos are both against the rules and big business in prison. Talented tattoo artists are well compensated and in demand. Tattoo needles are contraband. Fresh tattoos prompt searches. And infections. The warehouse guy accused me of allowing my clerks to commandeer the typewriter ribbons for tattoo ink, because we went through them so fast. A bit indignant, I invited him to come spend a day in the library and listen to the clatter of the typewriters in legitimate use. He did not take me up on the offer.

Tattoos in prison can be a kind of code. Specially trained investigators use them to determine whether particular inmates, because of their gang affiliation, must be kept separate, among other things. Tattoo markings can delineate a person's history of crime. Then there was the TV show wherein the inmate's tattoos secretly depicted an elaborate blueprint of and escape plan from the prison where he was incarcerated. I'm pretty sure that was fictional.

Various hospitals and groups on the outside specialize in tattoo removal, especially for former gangmembers who no longer want that kind of visible identification on their bodies. Getting a tattoo erased is much less fun than having it inked into the skin. I know this because my youngest daughter, in the months leading up to her wedding day, spent a lot of money and endured a measure of pain in the course of the removal of a tattoo from her early college days that she regretted. Fortunately, there are nonprofit organizations that provide this service free to people who are trying to move their lives away from their former gang membership.

I'm grateful that the fads of my youth, like hip-hugger bell-bottoms and tiny rose-colored glasses, were not permanently attached to our bodies. You can't outgrow a tattoo.

The Things They Left in Books

He was a little white boy. I found him in a book that came from R & R, in their sporadic delivery to the library of books that had been confiscated from inmates. The boxes from R & R were like Christmas morning to my clerks—new reading material!—but I always went through them first, in case they'd been seized because they contained banned or objectionable material. (Sacramento periodically supplied us with an unhelpful list of banned books. Little rhyme or reason seemed to apply in the selection process.) Most often, books were taken because each inmate was only allowed to have ten books in his possession at any one time, excluding legal necessities.

The little white boy was smiling in a standard school photo, showing his brand new large front teeth in the startling, new-arrival way of adult teeth in a child's mouth, but his eyes were focused just past the photographer. I imagined the photographer, taking her five-thousandth picture of a normal, run-of-the-mill kid, coaxing him to use the free plastic comb to bring order to his hair, saying the rote things that get kids to ease up and look slightly happy. She is not crazy about her job, but it's steady work—her employer is not going to run out of contracts for school pictures—and it comes with decent benefits. She'd rather be using her art degree to photograph sunrises or endangered tigers, but this kid will do for now.

Back to the kid.

He was wearing a red western shirt over a white tee shirt, against a blue school-photo background. I have dozens of versions of my daughters in this very setting, this very pose. He probably felt self-consciously all decked out, compared to a regular school day. In his red shirt he looked patriotic, an all-American boy.

The fact remained, though, that his photo ended up in a state prison, nestled in the pages of a book. On the back of the photo, someone had written, in blue ballpoint pen, "3rd grade / 8 yrs old." The writing was awkward and unformed, as though inscribed by a hand that normally has little use for handwriting. Whoever wrote it—whoever took the time to send his face to a man in prison—felt no need to write the boy's name. The recipient knew who he was.

Except now this child of God was in my top drawer in the prison library. Lacking an inmate's name or number, he would probably live in the back of this drawer forever, long after he was a boy of ten and a man of twenty, when he was old enough to form his own opinion of the man who kept his photo safe in a book. I said a furtive prayer that he did not follow the man to this place. Although I supposed that every inmate sitting in that library where I worked had looked just as young and hopeful in his own third grade school picture as this boy did.

This boy, however, possibly bore the secret burden of a father in prison and a mother handling his upbringing on her own, most likely in a financial position that made it hard to purchase even the cheapest school photo package.

He would be "3rd grade / 8 yrs old" forever in that photo in my drawer. In my mind he was the face of every kid whose father was incarcerated. I wished him every blessing as he grew. The kids whose school photos came in the prison mail were victims, too.

A short list of other items found in books, often functioning as bookmarks:

homemade string

plastic tooth flossers, used and unused

candy wrappers

important legal documents

free Bible pamphlets

trust account statements

mail order photos of sexy girls with cleavage and/or
     visible butt cheeks

old envelopes, faded and soft from handling

canteen receipts

pictures torn from the library's magazines

a postcard from Paris, breezily signed by a famous
     musician parent

any item that had been laminated

hair

Sports Fans

Sports are as American as apple pie, and in fact as global as competition, and in the fanatical love of sports the incarcerated population was no different from the rest of the world. Inmates on my yard had the opportunity to play such sports as tennis, softball, flag football, soccer, and basketball. They took part in tournaments and workout sessions and one-on-one games. The prison employed a staff member, the aforementioned Coach, who kept track of the equipment inventory in the gym and provided the rules and prizes for various sporting contests. (Coach's recreational duties also included choosing the movies that were shown on the prison channel, all of the available movies having been previously edited down to a PG rating.) The gym itself was a cavernous building that was always freezing cold, but it was a gift to be able to use it for recreation purposes, because there had been a period of several years, at the height of the statewide prison overcrowding crisis, when the gym had been turned into housing. Hundreds of inmates had inhabited a tight grid of double bunk beds. Living in the gym had reportedly been even worse than living in the dorms.

The inmates liked watching sports as well as playing them. The officers could be cruel or kind with the spectators who wanted to watch a big game, as they controlled the TV channels in the day rooms. Inmates were permitted to buy individual televisions, but the reception through the prison's antiquated antennae system in the mountains was spotty and somewhat terrible. The prison did not have cable, so channels like ESPN or the NFL Network were unavailable. You got what you got.

Although all gambling was illegal in prison, I was aware of fantasy football activity, because certain inmates on Monday mornings in the fall combed the sports section of the newspaper for statistics. Unlike fantasy football (or any other fantasy sport) on the outside, whose outcome is automatically calculated by a computer program or an app, the winners of fantasy football in prison were painstakingly determined by hand. Some very complicated math took place in the library. Money did not change hands, but the winning inmate could come into a bounty of soups.

As in society, sports activity in prison provided an outlet for physical energy and a showcase for athletic talent. Team sports also relied on cooperation and cohesion among men who might otherwise not get along. "The triumph of victory and the agony of defeat," as the old *ABC Wide World of Sports* television show used to proclaim, were in evidence in prison sports, too.

And spectator sports, as in society, were a common interest and an icebreaker. Sports gave people something to talk about and often something to bond over. Team affiliations could be shared or scoffed at, and big plays could be discussed and dissected. Sports could inspire passion and cement friendships.

Lastly, I must note that my clerks were good about disseminating the most important unwritten, but quickly learned, rule in the library: Never say anything bad about the Green Bay Packers, at least within earshot of their boss.

The Transformative Power
of the P Encyclopedia

Directly across from the front window of my office was the Reference Table, where patrons were directed to sit when they were perusing any reference book or any volume of our most recent *World Book Encyclopedia* set. This was because if we allowed these books to venture further out into the vast room of the library, pages disappeared, especially any pages with maps of California. From my window, I could see/survey/watch/keep track of the researchers at the Reference Table, and at least try to keep them honest.

On one particular day, I glanced up several times and saw an older gentleman who had checked out the *P* volume of the encyclopedia. English was his second language, and he paged through the book slowly. The cover that faced me sported a photo of a brightly colored parrot. It was the brightest thing in the room, the exotic plumage in stark contrast to the sea of faded blue shirts and blue trousers, the nondescript walls, the dark wood bookcases, the industrial tables and chairs. The parrot, the longer I looked at it, appeared almost in 3-D, as though it might burst free of its hardbound background and fly up to the high ceiling of the library. Every man in here, at one time or another, had yearned to do that, to fly free of the razor wire fence and keep on flying up through the clouds, up toward the sun, high above and away from this remote institution.

The man was happily engrossed in the world of *P* for hours, reading up on Parrots and who knew what else, Presidents or Plato or Persimmons or Phantom Fighter Jets. Watching him, I was struck anew by the power of the printed word. Every reader is familiar with that sense of wondrous displacement. If I could sit on my couch at home and be transported to another place, another time, another heart, another mind, another world, by the writing in a book, how much more precious would that escape be if I were incarcerated? I could see that the reader at the Reference Table was far away from the library, thinking freely, wholly involved in whatever *P* topic he was considering.

The prison mainly had a library for legal research, but the law was perhaps not as important as the moment of grace I was witnessing, thanks to the *P* volume. I felt as though I were observing a holy event, a testament to the fact that while the body could be imprisoned, the spirit had to give its permission to be put in chains.

Writing on the Inside

Alas, the poet was gone. He left for another institution. This was not his choice; when one is incarcerated, one goes where one is sent. His name appeared on a transfer list, his property was packed up, and he was transported by bus, along with the others on the list, by week's end. It was like he was never there.

I first got to know the poet when he asked me to proofread some of his poems before he sent them out to various editors. He spent part of every day at one of the library typewriters, so he was a familiar face. He had already received a few rejection slips, and as a fellow freelance writer, I shared my own large number of rejections. We got to talking about query letters and postage and self-addressed-stamped-envelopes and potential markets. That's when it occurred to me that the writers in the library might benefit from a writers' group.

Writing is a solitary act, but I knew that my writing had matured over the years with the help of writing groups and workshops and feedback from other writers. I asked the poet if he thought something like that might interest him. Being a dedicated writer, he agreed immediately. I asked some of the other library writers. There was the guy writing the fantasy novel, volume one of a projected ten volumes, who eventually asked permission to list the writers' group and me in his anticipated published acknowledgements. There was the guy writing a children's story to help children cope with death—not an easy task. There was the guy with the MFA in Creative Writing, whose searing essays on life in prison read rather as if Tim O'Brien had gone to prison instead of Vietnam. They signed the sign-up sheet. Another young guy asked me if he could come to the group. He hadn't ever written anything, but he might want to start. He asked if he could bring a friend. With the poet, that meant there were six writers at our first meeting.

We started with introductions and then a warm-up writing exercise. I gave each of them several sheets of loose paper in a folder, since the standard writing-group spiral notebooks are forbidden in prison. Then we wrote for five minutes about our earliest memory. The veteran authors jumped right in. The two new guys looked around nervously and then haltingly began to write.

For nearly five years, we continued to meet for an hour every Wednesday afternoon in the library. I got to listen to an astonishingly high level of writing.

"Like my father, I fathered a fatherless son," wrote one young man, twelve poetic syllables containing a world of trouble and hurt, as well as a succinct diagnosis of one of society's major maladies.

"We are the black sheep, shorn of reality," wrote an older gentleman, in another flash of insight, self-deprecating yet astute. I often found myself humbled to sit amongst a group of writers discovering the salvation inherent in the act of writing.

These were not writers pecking at a laptop or reading their verse from their iPhones; aside from a few stand-alone computers provided for shared use for legal research only and the staff computer in my office, the library existed in a land that technology forgot. These were writers with pencils and odd assortments of lined paper, who knew the mental click when the pencil leads the brain, who bravely scratched their way through pages and pages of words, discovering what they truly thought, away from the clang and posturing of prison life.

"Never again in my life will I have this kind of time to work on me," wrote an inmate who would soon go home and who intuited the therapeutic benefit of the well-filled journal. "I was gonna go after him. Thought I might have to put him on the ground. But then I thought: maybe he's just having a bad day," wrote one writer, in an inkling of the revelatory concept of empathy after thirty-odd years in prison. The subject matter for these writers was grit and rage, longing and injustice, and yet they would spend a long and gentle time thinking about a single word, a semicolon, a verb tense. The group members wore ill-fitting, prison-issue clothes and answered to a prison number and measured time in parole dates and conviction terms, and they were writers.

I mourned the poet's departure. He went to an institution that he'd heard was without typewriters, and he was dismayed at the prospect of having to mail out handwritten submissions, with handwritten apologies for his lack of professionalism. I didn't have the heart to tell him that his typewritten submissions must arrive on each editor's desk looking like they surfaced from a lost mailbag from the 1970s. I told him to keep hope in his heart and to write no matter what his available writing tools might be.

Other writers took the poet's place in the writers' group, as other inmates joined and then were gone, transferring and paroling and going out to court, or sadly, returning after committing a new crime. Prison was like Dorothy's observation of Oz: "People come and go so quickly here!" The writers group grew to include the young man who wrote poignant and beautiful raps on growing up as a lifer in prison from the age of fifteen and the poet who wrote textured, lonely couplets that inhabited the spacious world between despair and redemption. There was the Iraq War vet who wrote his way through rage and guilt, stunning us with the raw emotion behind his quiet delivery. There was the guy who had actually made his living as a television writer; everything he wrote was funny. He had a riff on the diceyness of offering literary criticism to hardened criminals: "I think you can cut back on the adjectives. Don't kill my family." There was the novelist whose saga, set in Russia in 1910, was about persecuted Jews and their fraught flight to America; his tiny writing covered every millimeter of his precious paper and his command of language was breathtaking. There was the fellow writing a zombie story set in Latino Los Angeles whose ear for dialogue was exactly on key. There was even the show-off who tended to write things for shock value, mostly about his balls, but I didn't give him the satisfaction of a reaction. All of life is raw material,

I'd tell the writers. Little is sacred or off-limits to a writer intent on squeezing meaning and truth out of real life.

The writers read their work and accepted suggestions and pondered praise. They laughed and sometimes cried. They proofread each other's pages. They steered each other to accomplished authors of pertinent genres to read, understanding that, as writers, the quality of our writing got better when we read good writing; after all, we were sitting in a library full of the works of great authors. I encouraged the writers to submit their work, to publish, so that the satisfaction of seeing their work in print could fill their hearts, so that they could take pride in something they did while incarcerated.

Before the poet left, he shared his news of three separate pending publications of his work. Other writers had successes in small magazines, unpaid but priceless, their first published clips under their imaginary belts. One day we may see one of their bylines in *The New Yorker*. One day these men will be released from prison. They will go back to whatever pieces of their lives will still have them, but they will go back as seasoned, thoughtful writers. Now that they possess the power of the written word, I hope that they will continue to write, as testimony to the act of writing as rehabilitation, as redemption, as rebirth.

"My life is on the write track," wrote one budding author, and I wasn't certain if the choice of the wrong homonym was intentional. Either way, it worked.

Getting the Written Word Out of the Prison

L ike all writers, the writers in the writers' group wanted their work to reach the public. Every writer wants the privilege of a reader. Once I heard the writer Margaret Atwood say, during a talk she gave at the *Los Angeles Times* Festival of Books, that "no one writes anything down without imagining a future reader, even if it is oneself further along in life." The circle of writing is only closed when the words are read.

Every writer maintains a healthy file of rejection slips, although in the outside world, these are now digital. A few of the writers in the group were finding that when they sent their work to magazines or book publishers, the formulaic rejection noted that submissions were only accepted via email. This left writers in prison behind. So when a national magazine that welcomed hard copy submissions by mail called for essays on the topic of "Breaking the Law," this invitation seemed right up our alley. We decided the group would send a mass submission. For some the topic was maybe too close to home, since only five writers in the group took on the challenge. Two weeks in advance of the magazine's deadline, our submissions were set to travel through the US mail with the hope of publication.

The group's entries were compelling, by which I mean harrowing. They were expressive and explosive, detailing both deeds and repercussions: getting busted for punching a stranger in the face, drinking to blackout and waking up in handcuffs, stealing a cop car, robbing a liquor store but not meaning to fire the gun. They had written honestly and credibly. I had edited and typed their work. They were relevant submissions, ready to go. I put them into the outgoing mail. We crossed our fingers and hoped for a positive response.

Except they never went out.

A mailroom worker flagged them as questionable. Emails regarding both their content and the permissibility of the endeavor went from the mailroom to the lieutenant to the watch commander to the investigative unit to the community resource manager to the principal of the education department. This cautionary process apparently took a few weeks. The principal stood up for the group, so I was not fired. But I had to tell the writers that their work hadn't made it to the magazine before the deadline. They were disappointed, even more so because they had not been rejected by an editor but blocked by the institution from consideration. It was yet another thing that sucked about being in prison.

But writers write. The failure was another lesson in perseverance. In the world of publishing, doggedness can be as essential as talent.

And these guys had both.

The Caged Bird

Most writers want to be read. We write solo, spending hours by ourselves, wrapped in words until our backs are stiff and we come up for air and realize the morning is gone. We are loners, and we are OK with that. But once the work is written and rewritten, polished and re-polished, we totally want someone to read it. And to be somehow affected by it. And to tell us so.

As a fellow writer, I could see that the writers who faithfully attended the writers' group and shared their work also craved the feedback that comes with publication. So I had an idea. I requested permission to put together a newsletter for the prison yard.

This was not as easy as it sounds. Permission required many steps, consisting of putting in a proposal and requesting the necessary supervisory signatures and waiting and waiting and waiting for approval, and then starting from scratch when my higher-ups got promoted and were replaced by new higher-ups. If there was one lesson I'd learned from years of freelance writing, however, it was persistence. Finally, the newsletter got the green light. Our group gave birth to *The Caged Bird*, a title cribbed from the great Maya Angelou's autobiography *I Know Why the Caged Bird Sings*, which in turn borrowed the line from an earlier poem called "Sympathy," by Paul Laurence Dunbar. Writers are thieves.

I decided to make it a quarterly newsletter, because it was going to take a lot of time out of my regular job duties. An accomplished writer named Feehan took on the role of in-mate-editor-at-large, a title he chose for himself. Thanks to the persuasive powers of the gregarious Feehan, the newsletter eventually included fiction, poetry, memoir, artwork, book reviews, graduation speeches, recipes for hot pots, informa-tional pieces, yard news, holiday notes, opinion essays, puz-zles, a few works in Spanish, inspirational quotes, advice, and original translations of several Psalms from Greek to English. Once Feehan went around the dorms soliciting submissions, we had plenty of material to fill our pages. There was an abun-dance of talent on the yard, just waiting to be noticed and encouraged.

Due to my limited desktop publishing skills, the masthead featured a fancy font, with free clip art of a bird in a cage on the left and a bird flying free on the right. Cheesy clip art separated articles, illustrated poems, and filled small blank spaces. The format was a two-column Word document with a border, printed on two sides and stapled together. Not exactly an award-winning design. Our first issue was two pages; in time it grew to sixteen pages. It was an amateur labor of love, but it was enough.

A byline appearing in *The Caged Bird* was the first time some of the writers got to go public with their talent. They were excited and nervous and proud. The feedback from the yard was positive, including the supreme comment that writers live for: "I read what you wrote, and I know exactly what you mean, man. I wish I coulda said it like that." The published authors sent copies home to their moms. The lifers included their published clips in their board packets. We often had to print a second run when we ran out of copies. I made sure to get the higher-ups' approval of each issue in writing, so that any controversial material, as well as my low-level butt, was covered.

Feehan was adept at convincing the artists on the yard to allow us to feature their work. I didn't understand their reluctance to be included in the newsletter—the writers were eager to be published—until Feehan enlightened me: the artists were used to being paid for their efforts. They created art as a commercial venture, and we didn't pay. Nevertheless, he secured beautiful and intricate art for our newsletter issues, most of which had to be scaled down in size and was hardly done justice by our copy machine. Feehan also badgered Ramon to share his patented recipes for the hot pot, the only cooking device allowed in the dorms. We called this column "The Incarcerated Gourmet." Popular dishes, whose ingredients were all available on the yard, included Sunday Stew, Jalapeno Summer Sausage Soup, and Manwiches.

Eventually, Feehan convinced me to stop calling *The Caged Bird* a newsletter, an identity he found too pedestrian. Thanks to him, we added the subtitle *Promoting Creative Arts in Prison*. My replacement at the library agreed to continue producing *The Caged Bird* after I retired. Sadly, that has not gone so well.

So I think of *The Caged Bird* as a golden moment in the story of the library. It did some people some good, me included. It was something different, difference being a much-appreciated quality within the monotony of prison life. One of the most prolific writers on the yard, whose writing grew and improved noticeably over time and whose work was featured in every issue of *The Caged Bird*, left me a note before he transferred to another facility: "Please remember who I've become and not who I was."

It's the best thank you I ever got.

History Being Made

n present day usage, the word "penitentiary" is a synonym for prison, a place where we house lawbreakers while they serve their sentences and pay their debt to society. Perhaps surprisingly, "penitentiary" derives from the Latin *poenitentia*, meaning repentance, or the desire to be forgiven. (Not surprisingly, so does the word "penitent," a person desiring the sacrament of "penance.") Once upon a time, a penitentiary was a place one could go to reflect on one's religious transgressions and to ask forgiveness of God. And in early America, a penitentiary was different from a prison in that its purpose was reform rather than punishment.

The history of incarceration is as old as time. From the story of God banishing Adam and Eve from Eden, in effect keeping them walled off from paradise, to the dungeons of the Middle Ages to the notorious Bastille in Paris to the penal colonies established on faraway shores to the prison-industrial complex of today, transgressors have been punished by separation from society. As soon as rules and laws were made, they could be broken. Repercussions followed naturally. Infamous people have done time: Al Capone, Charles Manson, the Manson women. Then there are the unjustly imprisoned, usually for political reasons: John the Baptist, the Count of Monte Cristo, Gandhi, Martin Luther King, Jr., Nelson Mandela, Vaclav Havel, the women of Pussy Riot. These are but a few examples of people who have been unfairly deprived of their freedom by the state. The overwhelming majority of inmates are not famous. Most of the inmates I worked with were neither wealthy nor connected nor well-educated.

Many of them, however, saw education as the way to break out of the pattern of poverty and lack of opportunity into which they had been born. They worked hard to educate themselves, especially in matters of the law, so that they could understand their cases and sometimes fight them. And they had their eyes on the kind of history that is made in small ways every day.

The California State Legislature's website offered email tracking alerts for Senate and Assembly bills as they made their way from the committee process to passage and then to the governor's signature. I signed up for any that pertained to criminal justice. The legal-minded inmates were always looking for an angle, and a change in the law could be life-altering, especially if its provisions were retroactive. Over my years in the library, the laws changed significantly, turning drug-related felonies into misdemeanors, treating adolescent criminals with special consideration for the fact that they were not adults at the time of their crime, reducing the sentencing enhancements that could add years and decades to a sentence, or declaring that those in prison on a murder charge could petition the court for resentencing if they'd been convicted as an accomplice to a murder rather than the actual killer. The bills the governor signed were often small blips on the evening news for society, but they were huge stories for prisoners. They could also cause seismic shifts in the prison population numbers, as well as add to the short-order paperwork that staff had to complete in order to accommodate earlier releases due to changes in sentences.

After a complicated-by-red-tape but ultimately successful campaign to get additional large bulletin boards installed in the library, we posted—with staples, not thumbtacks—any criminal justice news we could get our hands on. The local newspapers, national magazines, the internet, nonprofit advocacy groups, the department website itself—all were possible sources of such news. We provided accurate information with an eye toward dispelling rumors. Curiously, there were staff members who resented this attention to current events, who preferred that inmates be kept in the dark, devoid of hope and ignorant of their rights. The punitive mentality showed up in all corners of the prison.

My years in the library witnessed some real and substantive changes to the criminal justice system in California. A progressive government helped to change minds in the community, and the impact of public opinion on both policy and politics should never be underestimated. Awareness was growing of the acute need for treatment for the large percentage of mentally ill inmates, those who'd been incarcerated less for criminal activity and more for the inability to cope in society. The pendulum was slowly swinging from punishment to rehabilitation, from locking up to healing, profoundly affecting the lives of real people. Steps like abolishing the cash bail system and restoring the voting rights of ex-felons can advance society toward equal justice. Recent nationwide election results similarly point to the public's desire to reform a system that has failed so many. Hope and change, as they say.

The Geography of the Yard

Two a.m. to five a.m. is a lovely time," said Marcus. Marcus, an older African-American inmate with a statesmanlike peppering of gray in his beard and hair, had just turned in a book report. Living in a dorm of 160 grown men bunked by twos, he treasured the sliver of serenity available only to the night owls. He read in the wee hours when the rest of us, except for the first watch guards, were asleep. This "lovely time" was his favorite part of each twenty-four-hour cycle on the yard. "So much noise these youngsters make," he added, shaking his head as though considering the book he could write, *Fools Marcus Has Known.*

The yard encompassed the whole universe of each inmate incarcerated there: the dorms, the chow hall, the library, the chapel, the laundry, the canteen, Medical/Dental, Clothing, Visiting (with its anteroom full of human cages, where inmates were stripped and searched before and after visits, as well as confined for disciplinary or safety reasons), R & R (Reception and Release, the only way in or out for inmates), Control (the booth from which officers controlled staff access to the yard), the offices of the Sergeant on duty, the Lieutenant on duty, and the Captain (offices inmates do not want to be called to for any reason), the Correctional Counselors' area, the Parole Board room, the Gym, and the back area of the yard with a track for running and walking, basketball courts, tennis courts, chin-up bars, a few benches for sitting, the Native American sweat lodge, and a field used for playing soccer, softball, and flag football. That was pretty much it.

Periodically the yard underwent what I thought of as "Audit Fever." When state auditors—the "suits"—were expected, suddenly everything was painted and repaired. Broken things were finally thrown out or hidden. Fire extinguishers were inspected and restored to working order. A careful inventory of all chemical cleaners was constructed. A sergeant came to make sure that we dusted the shelves, waxed the floor, aligned the chairs, things we regularly did anyway. I knew an audit was coming when my missing floor tiles were replaced and a new, lit-up "EXIT" sign was installed over my back door in the same week.

The yard was both a physical setting and a metaphorical state. The yard ran on unwritten rules. The yard could be a harsh judge. The yard meant different things to different populations. For me, the yard existed outside the doors of the library. Conflicts and prejudices belonged out on the yard, not in the library. Closed mindsets and ignorant opinions were to be left out on the yard. They were unwelcome in the library. As far as I was concerned, the library was on the yard, but not of the yard. It was a place of light and learning. It was sacred ground.

The Geography of Hope

My everyday work in the library revolved around many lifers. They were the ones running the self-help groups and mentoring the younger men (or "knuckleheads") and putting together parole packets in the library. This last was like a full-time job in the months before a scheduled hearing. Lifers could mail their parole packets to the Board in advance of a hearing, so that the board commissioners could read up

on their parole plans and rehabilitative efforts before meeting
and evaluating the inmates face-to-face. Lifers with outside
resources could hire private lawyers who specialized in parole
hearings to represent them, but the cost was in the thousands
of dollars. Unless an inmate came from money, it was rare that
a family could scrape together this fee, and then at great sac-
rifice. Most of the lifers therefore had to make do with state-
appointed attorneys, who often represented more lifers than
they could possibly get to know or advocate for fully or passionately. Since they sometimes only met with this very important attorney once, lifers knew that they had to be their
own best promoter.

The consequences were real. In the past, board hearings
were already decided before they began: lifers accepted the
done deal that they would be denied parole. Or, if they were
somehow found suitable, the governor reliably would reverse
the board's decision. No one really sweated board hearings in
the old days, because they made no difference. They rubber-
stamped a lifetime of custody. Cultural and legal shifts, however, had made it more likely that a lifer would be found
suitable for parole and receive a release date if he could demonstrate that he was no longer a danger to society and that he
had realistic avenues to work and housing. Making these possibly life-changing plans involved a lot of research and correspondence, much of which was done in the library.

Many lifers, having spent decades in the prison system, had
nothing resembling a support network on the outside or even
family members to welcome them back into the fold. Their
parents had often passed away, and if they did have other
family members willing to take them in, chances are that the
board would frown on such an unstable or compromising
environment for someone returning to society. Paroling to the
home of someone with a history of drug abuse, for example,

was hardly a recipe for success. Lifers instead turned to transitional housing.

A viable parole packet usually included an acceptance letter from a known network of transitional homes in the area to which the inmate would be paroled. Transitional housing was a sort of rest stop on the way to freedom. Typically run by churches or nonprofit organizations, a reputable transitional home would include a safe place to sleep and eat in community with other recently-released lifers, job placement and other social services designed to help the men reintegrate themselves into society, mentors to help with a zillion other issues, like legal questions or even how to use a cell phone or public transportation, and access to 12-step programs to help those with substance abuse issues stay on the straight-and-narrow. A good transitional housing organization navigated a fine line between establishing necessary house rules and structure and allowing the men to begin to make their own decisions, between hand-holding and hands-off-ing. A lifer with this kind of proactive support from people who understood where he'd been and where he could dream of going was likely to succeed.

My husband and I became supporters of an organization called Francisco Homes in Los Angeles. In ten years, a group of industrious nuns turned one home into seven, and they said they could easily fill several more. There was a waiting list and a huge demand for their services. They estimated that they had housed and cared for nearly five hundred men so far and had seen no new arrests. That's right: zero new offenses. Men stayed with Francisco Homes for an average of sixteen months before moving on to more permanent situations. They had a safe place with people who supported them as they found work and reintegrated back into the community and who treated them with dignity and respect while holding them accountable for their choices. Several of the library clerks had passed through Francisco Homes on their way to freedom.

Working within the prison system and now keeping in touch with men who'd been released has given me endless bouquets of blessings. I have met living saints who work and volunteer with the formerly incarcerated, who believe that no one is disposable. I have seen men blossom in love relationships and in newfound careers. I've received letters and emails full of struggles—one clerk described how hard it was to adjust to the smell of cars and buses in the city after not being around exhaust fumes for over thirty years; another, the scary days of being homeless for a time—but also full of good news. After I retired, I had coffee with a former library clerk and realized that I was wearing a blue shirt, a color he might never wear again, and he was wearing yellow, a color not seen on an inmate. He was living with a very kind mentor who had visited him in prison and opened his home to him. He was applying for jobs far below what his experience and training would indicate, but the ankle monitor he had to wear limited his prospects. Nevertheless, he was happy. He was alive with the possibilities ahead of him, having relocated from the confines of prison to the geography of hope.

Prison doesn't always end with release: the mentality of prison must be overcome, and the reality of being a felon in our society presents many challenges and difficulties. Those of us who have never had to worry about such things can continue to be the face of compassion for people who are finding their way anew into society. Visiting the imprisoned is only one of the corporal works of mercy to which we are called. Accompanying those who have paid their debt to society is an extension of the calling to mercy. Supporting transitional housing and employment opportunities and reentry programs for the formerly incarcerated are a few concrete suggestions for action. Praying for all those involved in this life-giving work is another.

"Go and Do Likewise": The Future Is Now

A voice for the voiceless" describes St. Oscar Romero, the Salvadoran bishop who was martyred because of his work and advocacy for the poor. Archbishop Romero was a modern incarnation of the prophet Isaiah, a voice crying out in the wilderness. Throughout history, the voices for the voiceless have been ignored or ridiculed or condemned or silenced by the powerful, but the faithful are still called to speak.

The Gospel of Luke often shows Jesus directing his followers to practice radical compassion. This teaching is summed up by the question Jesus asks the lawyer who has just heard the parable of the Good Samaritan: "'Which of these three, in your opinion, was neighbor to the robbers' victim?' He answered, 'The one who treated him with mercy.' Jesus said to him, 'Go and do likewise'" (Luke 10:36-37).

Show mercy, Jesus urges us. Be a neighbor. Use your voice. I don't know that anyone is more voiceless than a prisoner.

We who have perfectly functional voices can be compassionate advocates for the voiceless in this age of public interest in prison reform. The principles of social justice require that we be merciful and giving, but we can also have an effect on God's kingdom here on earth by working in the political arena to change unjust systems and institutions.

Laws in California are changing for the better, and other states are implementing radical reforms to their correctional practices. Organizations like the Innocence Project, the Prison Law Office, the Marshall Project, the Vera Institute of Justice, and the Equal Justice Initiative provide voices for the voiceless within the labyrinth of the justice system. Groups like Homeboy Industries, the Anti-Recidivism Coalition, and Francisco Homes offer a safe landing and resources for those exiting the penal system.

Our prisons have the potential to be places of positive growth and change. Bringing American public opinion in line with a system based on rehabilitation rather than punishment, however, might be the tallest order in such a transition.

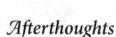

Afterthoughts

I kept a notebook in the library to help my faulty memory when I finally had time to write about these men with whom I worked, but when I look through its pages, I find that I only rarely recorded the verbal gems of each day. I wish I had been a better scribe. With affection, I share the following bits of levity and light.

Some Memorable Real-Life Quotes:

"The only man you can change is wearing your shoes."

"We step into tomorrow's shoes and see how they fit."

"I kind of burned the house down a little bit."

"They asked me to emcee at graduation: I'm the Master of Convicts."

"My gender is sci-fi." (When asked what writing genres appeal to him.)

"This book gives you insides on your behavior." (The Parole Board directs lifers to work on "insight" into their crimes.)

"I'm working on my self-extreme."

An inmate with no money on his books is called indigent: "How do I mail this? I'm indigenous."

"These copies are blurred! Your toner must need replacing! And they're crooked! These copies are all over the place!" (An inmate complaining about his photocopies of a medical appeal alleging a lack of treatment for his "very, very dangerously blurred vision.")

The Bottom Line: Loving the Unlovable

"Do not the tax collectors do the same?"
—Matthew 5:46

Some people are so easy to love. They are lovable from the moment they are born. They are pretty or sunny or funny or outgoing or kind or all of the above. You almost can't *not* love them.

"If you want to be loved, be lovable," goes the quote from that old soul Ovid. Sounds simple, yes? We like to think that love is an instinct, that we are made to love without any conscious thought, but loving may not always be instinctive. I believe, however, that you can be educated in love. From the moment a mother takes her baby to her breast, the education in love begins. Parents who feed and clothe their children, who make time to appreciate their children's milestones, who are fair and consistent in discipline: these are people who illustrate the many ways to teach love. Love that is given to a child is returned and learned and given to others, in a cycle of love and trust.

The hardest people to love are usually the ones who need love the most, who lack love in their lives. What if you don't know what love looks like or what love feels like? What if your trust has never been validated? If your own mother doesn't love you, how impossible must it be from day one to see yourself as lovable? If your own father doesn't care if he ever meets you, how will you ever think fathering is important? The cycle of unlovableness is nowhere more apparent than in prison. I've spent time with men whose mothers verbally abused them, whose fathers physically abused them, whose relatives sexually abused them, whose teachers gave up on them, whose friends turned on them. What kind of education happens in these instances?

The cycle of rejection and numbness is thus continued and passed onto the next generation. What is normal for some is not love, but self-protection. These are grown men who don't know how to trust others, who don't know how to receive love. How do we reach them? How do they reclaim their birthright of love? I think of them as members of the crowds to whom Jesus proclaimed the Good News, those for whom Jesus "had compassion . . . because they were troubled and abandoned, like sheep without a shepherd" (Matt 9:36). Therein lies the answer to the question of what Jesus would do: he'd have compassion. Whether we work in a prison or are simply concerned members of society, our brother Jesus is our role model of compassion.

And fearlessness. Jesus is not afraid, and he continually urges us not to be afraid. Fear keeps us from opening ourselves up and from exposing any vulnerability. Fear tells us to hang back so we don't look stupid. Fear prevents us from being our best selves, from trying anything new, or from putting ourselves into uncomfortable situations. Fear is the devil that paralyzes us. Fear insinuates that kindness is really a form of weakness. If we follow Jesus, though, we will not be afraid to be kind. We will not be afraid to be holy. We will reclaim our lives from fear. Maybe we will bloom and grow. Maybe we'll see others bloom and grow.

And love. Jesus is a lover, not a fighter, and he proves with his very life that love conquers all. Our hearts yearn to love and be loved, but we are masters at complicating the simple. A chaplain at the prison once asked Father Greg Boyle, the Jesuit priest who founded Homeboy Industries, for specific suggestions for programs that would aid in rehabilitating the incarcerated population with whom he worked. Father Greg sent back a short answer: "Bring love where none exists." The chaplain had hoped for something more concrete, a more nuts-and-bolts kind of approach to a daunting task, but that was all the help he got.

I think of those five words as a mission statement for life.

Pared to three words, just as profound: "Thy kingdom come."